Praise for *Be the Smarter You @ Workplace*

This book by Rasikraman Das is a groundbreaking book in the self-help genre. It combines spiritual wisdom and scientific research to present smart life-apps to transform you into a smarter and happier version of yourself. **—Dr. Vivek Bindra, Business Coach, Motivational Speaker**

Be the Smarter You @ Workplace is a remarkable book that seamlessly merges the rich corporate wisdom of our capitalist societies with the profound insights of sages throughout history. Backed by thorough research, this self-help gem delivers a wealth of actionable insights. What sets it apart is the ready-to-implement workbooks, empowering readers to apply these valuable teachings directly in their professional lives. **—Atul Bargaje, Leader of AI and Machine Learning Practice, Amazon**

A must-have manual that provides spiritually-grounded, ethical guidance in vital areas ranging from strategic planning through communication skills which are taught in elite business schools for guaranteed success in any work setting. **—Dr. Ravi Kathuria, Professor, Argyros School of Business & Economics, Chapman University, USA**

A confluence of solutions to management problems through the lens of Vedic wisdom, rationality and modern day business dynamics. A niche must read for everyone aspiring successful professional life! **—Dr. Shekhar Shukla, Pr**
IIM Indore

With my experience of coaching
I find this book to be a re
skills such as decision mak

management while incorporating spirituality in the discussion. The simplicity is nice. **—Namita Purohit, Life & Business Coach, Ex-Microsoft USA**

The book gives you usable nuggets to apply to your working style. It uses real examples from our history—Bhisma's explanation of 5 attitudes for success (Vigour, Resilience, Humility, Self-worth and Seizing opportunities) to help the reader understand how to be a better manager. **—Nidhi Agarwal, MBA, Product Manager, USA**

Thoughtfully structured with a lot of practical applications. The book gives multiple tools to leaders to introspect and organise their thoughts and actions to maximise their impact in their work area. **—Shekhar Saurabh, AVP Marketing, Godrej Consumer Products Limited**

This book is a very valuable toolbox of essential workplace skills to upscale your business to the next level. Every entrepreneur should have it. **—Ashok Nahar, Partner, A.R. Constructions**

BE THE SMARTER YOU @ WORKPLACE

Success Hacks for Business and Career Growth

RASIK RAMAN DAS

SIMON & SCHUSTER
London · New York · Sydney · Toronto · New Delhi
PARAMOUNT

First published in India by Simon & Schuster India, 2023

3 5 7 9 10 8 6 4 2

Simon & Schuster India
818, Indraprakash Building,
21, Barakhamba Road,
New Delhi 110001.

www.simonandschuster.co.in

Paperback ISBN: 978-93-92099-78-6
eBook ISBN: 978-93-92099-77-9

Typeset in India by SÜRYA, New Delhi
Printed and bound in India by Replika Press Pvt. Ltd.

FSC
www.fsc.org
MIX
Paper from
responsible sources
FSC® C016779

Simon & Schuster India is committed to sourcing paper that is made from wood grown in sustainable forests and support the Forest Stewardship Council, the leading international forest certification organisation. Our books displaying the FSC logo are printed on FSC certified paper.

Dedicated To

Bhagavan Shri Krishna

Who gave the original Workplace Excellence Class
to Arjuna at Kurukshetra

CONTENTS

BE THE SMARTER YOU @ WORKPLACE

Success Hacks for 10x Business and Career Growth

1. **Recipe for Success:** Discover the COACH formula for success
2. **Communication Skills:** Reduce transmission losses in communication and boost trust levels in relationships
3. **Team Building:** Teem in life with teamwork
4. **Art of Decision Making:** Apply the head-heart-hand approach to decision making
5. **Leadership 101:** Take your organisation on a roll with the chariot model of leadership
6. **Meeting Facilitation:** Let the brains deal with the storm, rather than create another
7. **Strategic Planning and Execution:** Aim for the sky with feet on the ground
8. **Dealing with Uncertainty and Change:** Master the trapeze act of change
9. **Work-Life Balance:** Transform the tightrope walking of multiple responsibilities into a cakewalk

Introduction

Organisations rule the world today. They inconspicuously shape the dreams of millions and invariably shape their destiny too. If you want to create an impact in the world today, you definitely need the vehicle of an organisation to take your idea to the masses. This book is especially meant for entrepreneurs and working professionals to help them build and run successful organisations, designed for making lasting impact. It is a *professional-excellence* sequel to the book *Be the Smarter You* which was focused on sharing life skills for *self excellence* and *interpersonal excellence.* In this book we shall share nine success hacks for professional development and business growth:

1. Everyone wants to taste the elixir of success in their business and profession. But not many have access to the secret recipe of success. Discover the COACH formula for success with the *Recipe for Success Hack.*

2. Words can unite people's hearts in love, but they also have the potential to slice their hearts to shreds. The words we speak contribute to where we go, what we achieve and who we become in life. Let us unravel the end-to-end process of communication from logging in with the right password to making meaningful transactions with the *Communication Skills Hack*.
3. Is your team experiencing I-llness or We-llness? Is the sum of the parts more than the whole in your team? Learn the five principles of team building with the *Team-building Hack.*
4. Making the right decisions at the right time is a hallmark of great leaders. Learn about the four obstacles in decision making—emotional frailties, rational negligence, people pressures and situational complexities and overcome them with the H^3 (Head-Heart-Hand) Approach with the *Art of Decision-making Hack.*
5. Isn't it an enigma that a big team/group/community/nation aligns and unites around someone who apparently appears to be just one amongst them? What is it about these leaders which inspires and aligns people positively? What are the social dynamics and organisational factors involved? Explore all this and more with the *Leadership 101 Hack.*
6. Meetings for an organisation are what the rudder is for a ship or the steering wheel is

for a car. They give direction and shape to the organisation. If they are misaligned or rusted, the organisation is headed for disaster. Learn the five principles for holding efficient and effective meetings with the *Meeting Facilitation Hack*.

7. Struggling to catch up with market trends and competitor tactics due to lack of a great strategy? Or distraught to see your brilliant strategic plans fail due to poor execution? Leaders need to think strategically and act promptly to help their organisations capitalise on opportunities and navigate through challenges. Aim for the sky with feet on the ground with the *Strategic Planning and Execution Hack*, in which we go over the seven-step process which seamlessly integrates strategic planning and execution.
8. The 21st century has been characterised by a climate of change with disruptive technologies rapidly changing the business landscape globally. Master the trapeze act of change with the *Dealing with Uncertainty and Change Hack*.
9. The balance of an aircraft is dependent on manoeuvers around its three axes—roll, pitch and yaw. The aircraft of life needs to be balanced around three axes—connection, community and contribution. Learn the art of balancing life to ensure a smooth ride even amid turbulent times with the *Work-Life Balance Hack*.

Businesses have gone through several stages of metamorphosis in the past 500 years from the colonial era to the industrial revolution era, to the production era, to the marketing era, to the infotech era and now we are moving into the disruptive technology era with technologies, such as AI, nanotechnology and block chain, revolutionising the way businesses have been conventionally done. As things around change at a fast and furious pace, businesses and the people working for them need to develop two critical competencies:

- Be flexible and agile to adapt to change;
- Be deeply anchored in timeless principles and fundamentals which can help them absorb and dampen the tremors of change.

As you can see in the chapter descriptions, this book brings together timeless spiritual principles with innovative systems and processes to offer you success hacks for achieving 10x business and career growth.

1. RECIPE FOR SUCCESS

Discover the COACH Formula for Success

We all are connoisseurs of good food. Culinary shows on the television—they have always enjoyed high TRP ratings. I am going to share with you a secret recipe for a much sought-after dish called 'Success'. A very interesting thing about the pudding of success is that the recipe remains the same whether you are cooking for one serving or a thousand, i.e., the same recipe can be followed for success in the life of an individual or for the success of a nation or a huge organisation employing thousands of people.

COMPETENCE

Please allow me to take you through a step-by-step procedure of preparing this pudding. Since success and winning are synonymous with sports, I would like to share examples of sportsmen who attained excellence by following this recipe. The first ingredient we need is a bowl full of competence. Competence is defined as the blend of knowledge, skills and experience.

From where can we procure competence? Is there any grocery store which delivers it? We are not born with competence, but we are all gifted with some latent talent within us. Albert Einstein is credited to have once said, 'Everybody is a genius. But if you judge a fish by its ability to climb a tree, it will live its whole life believing that it is stupid.' The crucial thing then is to identify that hidden talent within us lest we may end up being a tree-climbing fish. This requires prayerful introspection and benevolent direction. Usain Bolt is regarded as the greatest sprinter of all times—he is the only sprinter to win three consecutive Olympic golds (2008, 2012 and 2016) for 100m and 200m. However, as a child the Jamaican athlete was training to become a cricketer. The turning point came when his cricket coach, seeing his lightning run-up, suggested that he try track and field. His father also encouraged him to take up athletics instead of cricket and the rest is history. This is the importance of having coaches and well-wishers in our lives. They are at times able to notice things which may miss our attention.

The next riddle is, once identified how do we transform our talent into solid competence? We need to subject our raw talents to the fire of discipline. It is only with the fire of discipline that we can cook our talents into competence. Novak Djokovic is a case in point. He was ranked as the best tennis player in the world for 282 weeks and holds the highest match winning rate in the Open Era (84.3% wins). In 2016, he became the first player since Rod Laver (1969) to hold all the four grand slam titles at the same time. What is the secret of his success? In his own words, 'Success does not come at once. It is not a thing achieved overnight. It is the result of many, many, many years of working and trying to achieve goals.' Since childhood, Novak dreamt of being

World No. 1 and he persevered hard to crystallise his dreams. Novak Djokovic's training routine has helped him become one of the fittest athletes in the world. In the pre-season, he does four hours of tennis practice and two hours of physical workouts and yoga every day. Novak believes that ultimate success on the court is directly related to consistency and accuracy, as opposed to power and flashy shot making[1]. Novak has committed and disciplined himself to play a defensive game with an offensive attitude, which makes him the ultimate defensive player in the world. He has accomplished this vital goal by reducing his unforced errors, increasing his speed and stamina, and developing an all-court game by expanding his repertoire of shots. Rather than taking the risk of making an error while attempting to overpower his opponent (which is frequently tempting and always exhilarating), he assumes that every ball will return, and probably to the logical opening, and he is responsible for that next shot. That way, he reduces the risk of missing his shot and gives himself more time to reach the next ball. All this entails a great deal of practice, perseverance and discipline, beyond the display of spectacular talent and power.

The example of Arjuna becoming the best archer amongst the Kaurava princes is testimony to the magic that discipline adds to talent. Guru Drona was the military teacher for both the Kauravas and the Pandavas. Once Drona wanted to test how well his students were assimilating the military training. Drona put a wooden eagle on the branch of a nearby tree. To pass the test, the students were supposed to cut off the eagle's head with one arrow.

Guru Drona first asked Yudhishtira, the eldest of the Pandavas: 'Get ready, look at the eagle, and tell me what you are seeing.'

Yudhishtira replied: 'I see the sky, the clouds, the tree, the tree branch and the eagle sitting there.'

Guru Drona was not very pleased with this answer. He asked the same of all the students, one by one. All of them gave similar answers. Then came Arjuna's turn for the test.

Drona asked Arjuna: 'Get ready, look at the eagle, and tell me what you are seeing.'

Arjuna replied: 'I only see the head of the eagle and nothing else.'

Drona then asked a second question: 'If you are seeing the eagle, then tell me how strong its body is and what the colour of its wings is.'

Arjuna replied: 'I am only seeing its head and not the entire body.'

Guru Drona was very pleased with Arjuna's answer and asked him to go ahead with the test. Arjuna easily hit the eye of the eagle with one arrow because he had practiced concentrating on his aim single-mindedly. He passed the test with flying colours. Though some of the other students at Drona's academy, like Bhima and Duryodhana, were as talented as Arjuna, how is it that Arjuna ultimately surpassed them all in prowess?

Because of unrelenting practice and discipline. He sharpened his talent into cutting-edge competence, like no one else. Let us see how:

Arjuna's brother, Bhima, was a voracious eater. It was a dark new moon night, and Bhima felt really hungry in the middle of the night. He snuck into the kitchen, managed to find food, and started eating right there in the dark. This is a particularly special skill he had, one he had been practising ever since he was a kid. On this particular night, Arjuna was awake and he followed Bhima to the kitchen. When he saw his brother eating in pitch dark with perfect ease, it startled him. He had an insight: *'If Bhima can find his way to the kitchen, obtain food, and eat in such pitch darkness as if it is broad daylight, why can't I do the same with archery?'* Arjuna started practising even at night with great perseverance and eventually became the best of all archers.

Patanjali Yoga Sutra is the classic textbook of yoga. The first verse of the book says that the perfection of yoga begins with discipline: *atha yoga-anuśāsanam*. *Anuśāsanam* means discipline. Why just yoga? Without discipline success in any field shall remain only a dream. In the kitchen of life, bring in a bowl of your talents. Boil them over the fire of hard work and discipline. While the talent is being cooked over the fire of discipline to yield competence, let us prepare the next ingredient.

ATTITUDE

Ability or competence can bring one opportunities, but translating opportunities into success requires a crucial tablespoon of positive attitude. Whether one is an expert driver or an amateur one, the roads remain the same for both—what changes is the way the driver responds to the potholes or sudden sharp turns. When the going gets tough, the tough get going. It is attitude or mindset which sets the successful apart from the rest. In the Shanti Parva of Mahabharat, Bhishmadeva points out five negative attitudes which hinder one's ability to succeed:

1. Laziness
2. Lack of risk-taking ethos
3. Pride
4. Fear of public opinion
5. Procrastination/Waiting for right time

From another perspective, the converse of each of the above constitute five positive attitudes which can be seen as catalysts for success:

1. Vigour
2. Spirit of adventure/Resilience
3. Humility
4. Self-worth
5. Proactiveness/Seizing opportunities

Life is not a cakewalk. Challenges, impediments and reversals are going to greet you on your way. Among people with similar IQs and competence levels, winners stand out because of their ability to stay sane and apply themselves and their abilities even amidst chaos. When situations bowl bouncers and googlies on the unpredictable turf of life, only those people who manage to maintain their focus on the goal and keep persevering despite all odds eventually succeed. This calls for positive attitude.

Let me tell you the story of two of the most talented batsmen Indian cricket has produced to demonstrate that attitude was the differentiating factor which made one of them stand out. Sachin Tendulkar was 15 and Kambli was 16 when they put together a partnership of 664 runs in a domestic cricket match, in which both scored triple centuries. Very soon, the duo debuted for the Indian team in international cricket. Both were doing well and Kambli even became the fastest Indian to score 1000 runs in test cricket. He took just 14 innings to achieve this feat. However, the 1994–95 season test series against West Indies highlighted their diverging career trajectories. The pitch at Wankhede Stadium in Mumbai showed signs of being unprepared and the ball behaved erratically from day one of the match. To add to the vagaries of the pitch, the Windies fast bowlers, led by Courtney Walsh and Kenny Benjamin, were tearing in at the speed of lightning, sending down thunderbolts. Vinod Kambli looked perturbed with the unpredictable pace and was not anywhere near convincing in either of his innings. Sachin, on the other hand, appeared unfazed and composed and made it look extraordinarily easy to play. He struck convincing boundaries all over the ground and his score of 85 runs in the second innings proved to be a match-winning one. Though possessing similar batting competence, Sachin had the edge over Kambli because of his ability to calm his nerves and stay positive. Sachin went on to play for 24 years while Kambli disappeared from the international circuit shortly after as he failed to live up to the success he had achieved early in his career.

A sparkling example of positive attitude in the corporate world is that of Brian Acton, the co-founder of WhatsApp. Brian applied for a job at Twitter and Facebook in 2009, after he left Yahoo. Both the companies rejected him but his response to the rejections is worth noticing:

> Got denied by Twitter HQ. That's ok. Would have been a long commute.
>
> —Brian Acton (@brianacton) May 23, 2009

> Facebook turned me down. It was a great opportunity to connect with some fantastic people. Looking forward to life's next adventure.
>
> —Brian Acton (@brianacton) August 3, 2009

Leaving these rejections behind, Brian Acton, along with Jan Koum, went on to develop WhatsApp, which became world's most popular messaging application by 2015 and has over 2.25 billion users globally as of June

2023. Social media giant Facebook spent a whopping $19 billion to buy WhatsApp in February 2014.

You may now be wondering how to acquire the super positive attitude of Sachin Tendulkar and Brian Acton. Let me share a key principle here. Attitude is synonymous with energy. Positive attitude is basically positive or bright energy and negative attitude is essentially negative or dark energy. People with negative attitude use their energy against themselves or against the society. For example, a criminal or a short-tempered person also has a lot of energy but has it directed improperly. If you want to cultivate a positive attitude, you essentially need to plug into positive energy. How? By being in touch with sources of positive energy such as meditation, biographies of great people, spiritual books, association with people who carry positive energy, a lifestyle of goodness, etc. and also by unplugging from sources of negative energy such as backbiting, fault-finding, media rooms blaring (heart) breaking news every minute, addictions, violence-laden shows and cinema and the like. Are you ready to plug into positivity and unplug from negativity? Add a tablespoon of positive attitude to the steaming soup of competence and I am sure, you can now begin to smell the aroma of success.

CHARACTER

But wait a minute, the recipe is not yet complete. One final ingredient which shall add soul and give life to the pudding is the sweetness of character. Success seized at the cost of one's soul or human spirit is neither palatable nor sustainable. The world is disillusioned with such hollow shells of success. Martin Luther King, Jr once said, 'Our scientific power has outrun our spiritual power. We have guided missiles and misguided men.' Success in the hands of virtuous people is a boon, but in the hands of exploitative people, it becomes a bane. Universal values of selflessness, service, sacrifice, humility, gratitude, compassion and empathy give sweet flavour to the pudding of success.

Let me tell you the story[2] of an athlete who won by willfully losing a race—he won hearts by choosing honesty over victory. Kenyan runner and Olympic bronze medalist, Abel Mutai, was leading the cross-country race at an event in Burlada, Navarre, in December 2012. He was only a few metres from the finish line, but got confused by the signs and stopped, thinking that he had finished the race. A Spanish runner, Ivan Fernandez Anaya, was right behind him and, realising what was going on, started shouting to the Kenyan to keep running. Mutai did not speak Spanish and so could not understand what was being said.

Ultimately, Anaya pushed Mutai to victory. He said that he didn't deserve to win and chose honesty over victory.

A reporter asked Anaya, 'Why did you do this?' He replied, 'My dream is that one day we can have some sort of community life where we push ourselves and help each other win.' The reporter insisted, 'But you could have won!' Ivan looked at him and replied: 'But what would the merit of my victory be? What would be the honour of this medal? What would my mother think of it?'

If we ingrain this ethos of cooperation within our communities and workplaces, we could accomplish far greater successes sticking together, than what we can with our individual efforts while pulling each other down. Biologist and theorist, Edward O. Wilson, who is known for his studies of ants and bees, has shown that our evolution from a tribal into a global society increasingly calls for compassionate and cooperative approaches over callous and competitive ones to human interaction.[3] Wilson says that our 'selfish activity' in interpersonal relations is a curse that hampers success at all levels where groups of humans interact. Wilson contends that selfishness is innately dysfunctional in our highly interconnected societies and world today. He proposes to replace the axiom of 'Survival of the Fittest' to 'Survival of the Kindest'.

In today's wealth-driven world, the value of anything is measured in terms of its financial worth or ramifications. This is probably why noble values such as truthfulness, integrity, compassion, etc., are neglected because they don't have a bank account and cannot be listed on the stock exchange. And since they are not valued, they are not emphasised or worked on in the social order. However, if we wish to assess the value of these values in terms of their monetary clout, we'll be surprised. Let us look at a couple of case studies.

In order to avoid the cost of adhering to rigorous emission standards, Volkswagen came up with a clever idea—the company put a special type of defeat device in about 11 million of its diesel-powered cars to detect when those cars were being tested for emissions and change their results. But when this so-called 'diesel dupe' was discovered in September 2015, it wound up being far more costly for the company than simply following the rules. In the U.S. alone, Volkswagen was forced to recall more than 5,00,000 vehicles and pay about $25 billion in fines. But more severely, the brand lost trust in its customer base. The cost of honestly following the emission norms would definitely not have been this much. In essence, honesty earns a position for itself by its own merit in society and even, as evidenced here, in businesses.

Another riches to rags story is that of Enron Energy which was named 'America's Most Innovative Company' by *Fortune* magazine every year from 1996 till 2001 until its real innovation of forgery in accounting statements came into light. The company was using mark-to-market accounting to make itself appear more profitable than it actually was, while simultaneously hiding any losses in shell companies. When the truth was discovered, Enron's stock plummeted from $90 per share to 65 cents in four months, before dropping to a few cents per share. While the company took years to become the seventh-largest company in the U.S., it became bankrupt in a matter of months, after the fraud became public. Enron entered bankruptcy on 2 December 2001. That is how much honesty is valuable. Let us try to look into the financial equivalents of some of the universal values in the society:

Value of Honesty = Cost of Corruption

- Cost of corruption is at least $.6 trillion, or 3% of the global GDP as per UNO.
- According to the World Bank, businesses and individuals pay more than $1 trillion in bribes each year.
- Indian-owned Swiss bank account assets are worth 13 times the country's national debt.

Value of Self-restraint = Cost of Substance Abuse

- Drug and alcohol use in the U.S. alone costs $1.45 trillion in economic loss and societal harm annually (1.5% of World economy).
- Globally, alcohol results in 3.3 million deaths each year.
- 2.6 lakh people die annually in India due to alcohol consumption because of liver cirrhosis, cancer or road accidents
- Even after adjusting for tax receipts from the sale of alcohol, alcohol poses a net economic loss of ₹97,895 billion ($1506 billion). This amounts to an average loss of 1.45% of the gross domestic product (GDP) per year to the Indian economy.

Value of Gratitude and Relationships = Cost of Broken Families

- Children raised by single parents or parents in unstable relationships show a 8.2 times higher probability to present emotional or behavioural problems than children raised in stable, two-parent families, according to a ten-year longitudinal study by Hanninghofer et al.
- A survey conducted among India's young population (aged 15–34 years) in 2017, revealed that 12% of the youth reported feeling depressed often, and 8% said they felt lonely quite frequently.
- Need for senior living may rise to around 10 lakh beds in the next 10 years, which is a ten-fold increase over the current base implying a compounded increase of ~25% annually each year.

Value of Non-violence = Cost of Crime and Wars

- The economic impact of violence to the global economy was $14.76 trillion in 2017, in terms of PPP (Purchasing Power Parity). This is equivalent to 12.4% of the GDP.
- Violence cost the Indian economy a whopping $1.19 trillion (over ₹80 lakh crore) last year in constant purchasing power parity.

The above statistics is a just a sample which demonstrates that an investment in training and ingraining these qualities in the society will not only be spiritually uplifting but also financially rewarding. Thus, it is time now to add a couple teaspoons of the sugar of character to the pudding. This is how the recipe of success should look like:

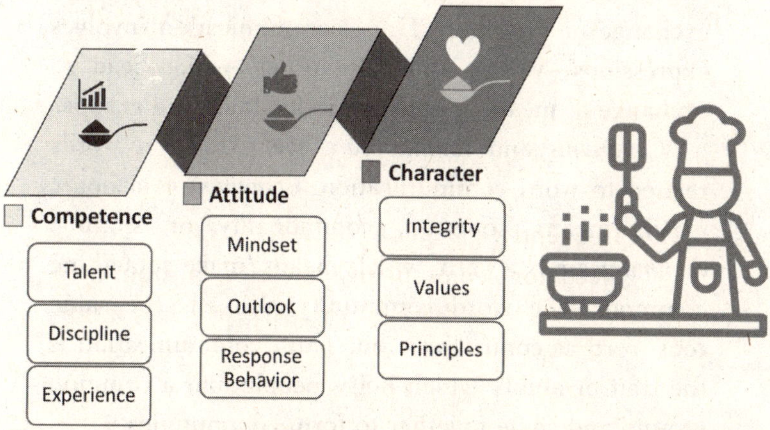

The Recipe for Success

Once the sweetness of character permeates through the entire pudding, it is ready to be served. Success is nothing but a seamless blend of these three ingredients: Competence, Attitude and Character. I call this the COACH formula or COACH recipe for success where Co stands for Competence, A stands for Attitude and Ch stands for Character. With this recipe in hand, I am sure you will be able to cook and taste the sweet dish of success in all your endeavours.

2. COMMUNICATION SKILLS

Reduce Transmission Losses in Communication and Boost Trust Levels in Relationships

The American Management Association gives a succinct yet profound definition of communication: 'Communication is any behavior that results in an exchange of meaning.' Thus, communication involves expressions—verbal and non-verbal—which lead to exchange of meaning between individuals and groups.

Communis and *communicare* are two Latin words related to word communication. *Communis* is a noun, which means common, commonality or sharing. *Communicare* is a verb, which means 'make something common'. The word community also has the same root word as communication. Thus, communication is the trait or ability which helps people find a common ground and come together to form communities.

Man is a social animal because of his evolved ability to communicate. Mankind has developed numerous languages to communicate with one another. Further, with the rise of technology, we have access to countless mediums of communication, and physical distance is no longer a barrier now. However, communication is a double-edged sword. Misunderstanding and miscommunication have led to bitter conflicts, feuds, riots and wars at all levels in the society. The evolved ability to communicate, if not used appropriately, can cause great damage. If we observe our lives and our surroundings, we can easily see proof of this. In general, everyone tends to love children and pets even though they don't speak any formal language. We tend to understand them without any exchange of words. However, we find misunderstandings and conflicts brew over trivial matters between people boasting of evolved vocabularies and oratory skills.

Words can unite people's hearts in love, but they also have the potential to slice their heart to shreds. Words can flood our hearts with joy, but they can also create a tsunami of anger. Words can create boundless motivation, but they can also discourage and demoralise us. The words we utter can cause us to seize or lose opportunities. Words can create synergy and schisms. They can inflict and heal wounds. The words we speak contribute to where we go, what we achieve and who we become in life. Thus, communication is a powerful tool that can determine our destiny and experience in the journey of life. Interestingly it takes only about a year to learn to speak but it can take one a lifetime to learn when to speak, when not to speak, what to say and how to say it. Let's try to equip ourselves with some important principles and practices for good communication.

COMPONENTS OF COMMUNICATION

In a way, everything we do is communication. Communication is a package deal. It originates at the level of the mind, is articulated through our speech, reflected in our body language and corroborated through our actions. Psychologists say that a major portion of our communication is transferred through the non-verbal medium which comprises of body language, tone, etc., whereas actual words spoken may carry only a portion of the message. There are three components of communication.

Thoughts (*Manasa*)

Feeling the 'vibes' of a room or a person is a common human experience. Studies have shown that humans tend to intuitively sense emotional energy emitted by other people. If they perceive vibes of goodwill, they will orient themselves favourably for the forthcoming communication. On the other hand, vibes of suspicion and distrust result in people withdrawing themselves, even though the verbal message may be welcoming. This means that though communication is associated with the usage of words, it can happen even without any formal exchange of actual words. How? Through the subtle language of thoughts. Thoughts are the seeds of words. Watch your thoughts, they become words. Let me introduce you to the universe of thoughts which eventually manifest into words.

Vedic texts explain that sound or communication exists and is relayed at four levels—each subtler than the previous. Out of these four, only one is formally detectable and audible, whereas the remaining are at the level of thoughts. *Vaikhari* is the palpable and audible form of sound which we conventionally use for vocal or written communication. Subtler than *Vaikhari* is *Madhyama* which literally means the bridge or transitory phase and is basically the mental facsimile of spoken words. It is the intermediate stage of thoughts between our abstract consciousness and our articulated speech. It is something like the complete rehearsal of a speech in the mind before it is uttered vocally. Your thoughts and memories which are constituted of whole words comprise *Madhyama*. Subtler still is *Pashyanti* which is wordless thoughts—these are flash thoughts or mental imagery and are the seeds which sprout into *Madhyama* and *Vaikhari*. *Pashyanti* refers to visualisation or imagery and so the sound at this level is constituted of raw feelings and images. When you meet a dear friend after a long passage of time, when you come across a breathtaking landscape or when you get the news of the sudden departure of a relative, you are not even aware of the thought photons crossing your brain in those split seconds. You simply experience and feel the moment as a witness. Eventually as you gather yourself or later reflect on the incident, you can think and articulate the experience in terms of words. Let me give another example. You are designing a poster and are stuck with choice of fonts and then a sudden epiphany takes over you and you recall the visual image of a font and you intuitively know that that is the font you need to use even if you have not recalled the name of the font. After a little effort, you recall the name of the font and apply it. As they say, lightning comes before thunder and so imagery often comes before words. This is the reason *Pashyanti* comes before *Madhyama*. Probably because we intuitively think in terms of pictures, therefore, a picture speaks more than a thousand words. The subtlest of all sounds is *Para* which is transcendental to the previous three states. It comes from the spiritual realm and goes beyond material thinking and feeling to manifest the state of pure existence. While the other three levels of sound make their way in our life outside-in, this one goes inside-out that is, we generally learn sounds and their meanings from the world around us but the *Para* sound constitutes spiritual realisations which occur in the world inside us. These four states of sound have been said to originate from different *chakras* or energy centers in our body. *Para* corresponds to spiritual sound and originates in the *Muladhara* or root chakra, *Pashyanti* corresponds to emotive sound and originates in the *Manipuraka* or navel chakra, *Madhyama* corresponds to intellectual sound and originates in the *Anahata* or heart chakra and *Vaikhari* corresponds to physical sound and originates in the *Vishuddhi* or throat chakra. Subtler the level of the sound, more difficult it is to invoke or manipulate it. However, if we master the subtler levels of sound, we can positively manoeuver external levels of sound easily. Mastery on our *Madhyama* thoughts can lead to mastery of our *Vaikhari* communication. There are several meditational practices which can help one awaken deeper levels of awareness, so that we can work on our communication right at the root of it in the form of subtle thoughts.

Words (*Vaca*)

Let's talk more about the nuances of our verbal communication or *Vaikhari.* There is a lot of putrid junk floating in the ether on account of polluted speech in the form of falsehood, hate speech, duplicitous speech, slandering, etc. In the Bhagavad Gita, Lord Krishna recommends that we install three filters in our speech so as to minimise speech pollution. These three filters are: Is my speech truthful *(satyam)*, is it pleasing *(priyam)* and is it beneficial *(hitam)?* These filters will ensure that we don't speak words which we may regret later on in our life.

Truthful *(satyam)*: We should endeavour to be truthful to the best of our knowledge. Truthfulness of speech establishes the credibility of the messenger and his/her message. The following are characteristics of truthful speech:

- **Correct:** The speaker should pay attention to the correctness and authenticity of the message. Many times, the information we pass on is based on hearsay without the confirmation of the authenticity of the original source, leading to confusion, distrust and rumors.
- **Consistent:** Emphasis and consistency are important factors of good communication and help in developing clarity and trust. If different things are equivocally spoken of at different times, people shall find it difficult to trust you. On

the other hand, if the same message is repeated and emphasised consistently, it adds weightage to the message and creates a lasting impression in the minds of the people. In today's day and age of short attention spans, it is crucial that essential messages are repeated and emphasised regularly. It is said that a good orator tells the audience what he is going to speak about, then he elaborately presents his message and towards the end reminds the audience about the message he has just delivered. Upholding promises and commitments are also aspects of truthful speech, which imply that you mean what you speak.

- **Complementary:** Communication is a two-way process. Great communicators hear more than they speak. Without hearing from others, one will not be able to get a holistic perspective and will end up passing judgements. We shall carry uninformed and biased opinions about people and situations. The willingness to listen with open ears, understand with an open mind and accept with an open heart is the hallmark of a leader.

Pleasing *(priyam)*: Words spoken with a pleasing disposition help open the ears and hearts of our audience to receive our message.

- **Cordial:** The speech should be pleasing and cheerful as far as possible. People are naturally drawn to a person whose speech is respectful and cordial.

- **Concise:** The part of the brain used for processing new ideas, called working memory, is very small and can easily get overwhelmed if loaded with lot of information. Try to present essential information in as few words as possible, else you will lose your audience.
- **Clear:** Though the message should be concise, it should not be so at the cost of clarity or completeness. It should not be vague, abstract or equivocal, else it may lead to confusion or irritation in the listener. Clarity, completeness and conclusiveness are important characteristics of good communication as they eliminate confusion and give direction.
- **Contextual:** Reference to context is always essential in communication. The message should be articulated considering the time, place, situation and the person being addressed. Context also involves being considerate and sensitive to the receiver of the communication.

Beneficial *(hitam)*: Words are precious. Our words shape and reflect our personality. We shouldn't waste them by indulging in gossiping, complaining or backbiting and ensure that what we speak has beneficial consequences at the individual or social levels.

- **Constructive:** An important question to ask oneself before saying anything is, 'Will my words be beneficial for my audience and myself?' If a certain piece of information, though true, is detrimental or discouraging for an individual, we can abstain from sharing it with them. When we have to correct someone, we can do it in a constructive way so that they are uplifted and not discouraged.

- **Compelling/Cause-driven:** The communication should be able to galvanise people to come to a consensus for a shared, sacred cause. The message should communicate a compelling purpose translating into an ardent call for action.

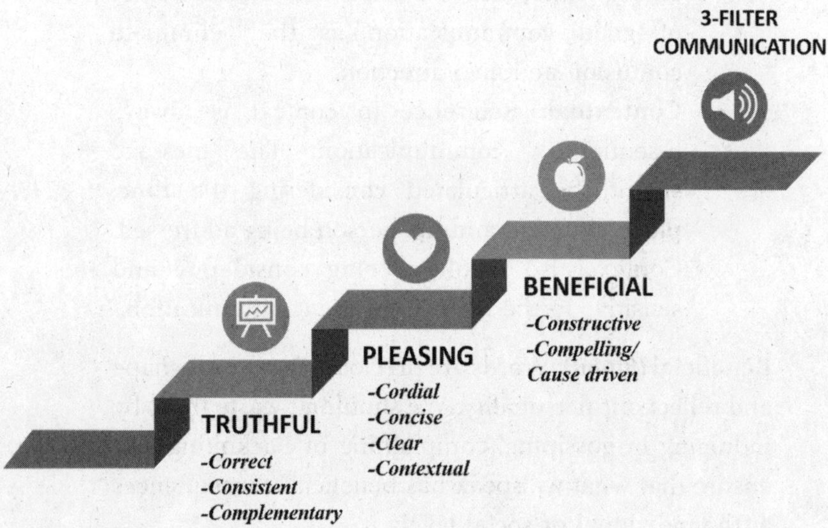

Actions (*Karmana*)

It is said, 'Actions speak louder than words.' People not only hear what you say but also observe what you do and form their opinions and decisions based on that. One's actions should be in congruence with one's thoughts and words, else one's words will lose value. A lot of communication is encrypted in body language too. If you say that you are interested in hearing the other person but intermittently keep looking at the watch and sit in a laidback manner, the other person will not feel inspired to express himself/herself.

Ultimately one's thoughts, words and actions should be aligned with each other. An ancient Indian wisdom text, *Padma Purana*, underscores the importance of the quality of integrity:

manasy ekam vacasy ekam karmany
eka mahatmanam |
manasy anyad vacasy anyat
karmany anyad duratmanam ||

Great people are those whose thoughts, words and actions are aligned whereas cripple-minded people are those who think or believe something, say something else and do something else.

PROCESS OF COMMUNICATION

Communication is a paradigm more than a process which means that it has more to do with mindset than verbal expressions. If you operate with the paradigm of valuing open and transparent communication, everything else will fall in place and your message will go through to the other person seamlessly. However, communication can be even more effective if it is riding on an effective vehicle. There are three stages in the process of communication:

- Establish Connection
- Exchange Communication
- Engage Cooperatively

Establish Connection

If you are not connected to the wifi you can neither upload nor download any data. If your cable isn't properly plugged into the switchboard, you can't expect your device to get charged. For a transaction of any sort to take place between two entities, we need the prerequisite of a proper connection. Similarly, the flow of communication between two people cannot begin unless there is a good connection. Therefore, the first and foremost step in communication is that of establishing a connection. In fact, a good connection made means half the battle won. Here is a story which shall help us appreciate the role of connection in communication:

A saint asked his disciples, 'Why do people shout in anger? Why do people shout at each other when they are upset?'

His disciples thought for a while. One of them said, 'Because we lose our calm, we shout.'

'But, why shout when the other person is just next to you?' asked the saint. 'Isn't it possible to speak to him or her with a soft voice? Why do you shout at a person when you're angry?'

The disciples gave some other answers but none satisfied the saint.

Finally he explained, 'When two people are angry at each other, the distance between their hearts increases a lot. To cover that distance and hear each other, they feel the need to shout. The angrier they are, the stronger they will have to shout to hear each other over that great distance.'

Then the saint asked, 'What happens when two people have a connection of love and respect? They don't shout at each other but talk softly. Why? Because their hearts are very close. The distance between them is very small...'

The saint continued, 'When the connection between the people is even stronger, what happens? They do not even need to speak, they simply glance and the other person understands. Finally, they need not even indicate, they understand each other's heart and do the needful without even being told.'

Thus, if people are connected with love and respect, communication is not difficult. American therapist and motivational speaker Sean Stephenson, says, 'Communication is merely an exchange of information, but connection is an exchange of our humanity.' We shall discuss three principles which shall help you establish that connection:

- Respect
- Reach Out
- Relate

Respect

Respect is like the circuit breaker in a relationship. Disrespect disconnects us. It causes the connection to trip. If you cannot respect, you cannot connect and consequently cannot communicate. When people perceive disrespect, they retract and insulate themselves from any further contact. Just like when a tortoise senses danger it retracts its limbs within its hard shell, people also retract from a relationship when they perceive disrespect. Without respect, the two sides may end up talking *at* each other, rather than talking *to* each other. Let us examine an anecdote to understand that when we enter into a conversation without respect, it potentially leads to miscommunication and misunderstanding. It is a fictional conversation being relayed on a Marine VHF radio system:

Canadians: Please divert your course 15 degrees to the South to avoid collision.

Americans: Recommend you divert your course 15 degrees to the North to avoid a collision.

Canadians: Negative. You will have to divert your course 15 degrees to the South to avoid a collision.

Americans: This is the Captain of a US Navy ship. I say again, divert YOUR course.

Canadians: No, I say again, you divert YOUR course.

Americans: This is the aircraft carrier, the second largest ship in the United States' Atlantic fleet. We are accompanied by three destroyers, three cruisers and numerous support vessels. I demand that you change your course 15 degrees North—I say again, that's one five degrees north—or countermeasures will be undertaken to ensure the safety of this ship.

Canadians: **This is a lighthouse. Your call!**

Reach Out

In order to connect, you need to reach out to where the object of your communication is. Enter the physical, social or digital space where they are located. You may not want to stay in that space forever but at least to get the communication across, you need to enter that space. You cannot expect to connect to people while being cocooned in your own shell.

Relate

The most important aspect of establishing a connection is the ability to relate with your audience. You need to talk to them in their language—both literally and figuratively. Nelson Mandela said, 'If you talk to a man in a language he understands, that goes to his head. If you talk to him in his language, that goes to his heart.' Different people understand different languages. You cannot connect to a teenager using the same language with which you are able to connect to your business partner. In order for people to relate to you, they should find your message to be relevant to them. You need to step into their shoes, understand their perspectives and address their needs, interests and concerns.

If you are able to relate to others, the opposite will also hold true, i.e., they will also be able to relate to you. King Dashrath's ministers highlight Shri Rama's empathetic nature as a reason for him being the unanimous choice of the citizens for becoming the next king, 'Rama feels very sad towards afflictions of men; and feels delighted in all functions celebrated by people on the occasions of childbirth and the like, just as their own father does. Rama, who talks smilingly, protects righteousness in all ways. Rama duly performs beneficent deeds. After returning from battle, Rama goes to the citizens and enquires about their well-being as though they are his own kinsmen, like a father asks his sons. He asks about their wives and children, about their spiritual well-being, about their servants and students, always completely as per the due order. Due to all these qualities, he is most dear to all the citizens and is thus fit to lead them.'

Different people see the same thing from different perspectives based on their experiences. On a lighter note, let us see how the same object is perceived differently by different people:

A language instructor was explaining to her class that French nouns, unlike their English counterparts, are grammatically designated as masculine or feminine. Things like 'chalk' or 'pencil', she described, would have a gender association although in English these words were neutral.

Puzzled, one student raised his hand and asked, 'What gender is a computer?' The teacher wasn't certain which it was, and so divided the class into two groups and asked them to decide if a computer should be masculine or feminine. One group was comprised of the women in the class, and the other, of men. Both groups were asked to give three reasons for their recommendation.

The group of women concluded that computers should be referred to in the masculine gender because:

1. They have a lot of data but are still clueless.
2. They are supposed to help you solve your problems, but half the time they ARE the problem.
3. As soon as you commit to one, you realise that, if you had waited a little longer, you could have had a better model.

The men, on the other hand, decided that computers should definitely be referred to in the feminine gender because:

1. No one but their creator understands their internal logic. The native language they use to communicate with other computers is incomprehensible to everyone else.

2. Even your smallest mistakes are stored in long-term memory for later retrieval.
3. As soon as you make a commitment to one, you find yourself spending half your paycheck on accessories for it.

If we want to connect to people with different perspectives, we will need to understand and appreciate them first, else we will continue operating in silos or as disconnected islands.

Exchange Communication

Establishing a connection is the beginning of communication. We need to actually go ahead and communicate. You cannot sit idle and assume that the other person is on the same page. George Bernard Shaw, the famous Irish playwright, set us straight on this when he said: 'The single biggest problem in communication is the illusion that it has taken place.' We shall discuss three principles which shall help us make a meaningful exchange of communication:

- Own Responsibility
- Organise Dialogue
- Open Up

Own Responsibility

There are two styles of communication:

- The Monkey type: Ownership of communication lies with the audience

- The Cat type: Ownership of communication lies with the communicator

Let me explain this. If you have ever seen herds of travelling monkeys, you must have keenly observed how the infant monkey tightly clasps onto its mother's belly as the mother-monkey jumps from one tree or building to another. The onus for staying connected lies on the infant monkey. In the monkey style of communication, the speaker is focused more on unshelving his/her message without much consideration of how much the audience is able to grasp it. In contrast to this style, the cat very carefully carries its kitten with its mouth, while the kitten revels in the safety of the mother's grip. In the cat style of communication, the speaker owns up to the responsibility of conveying the message in a way that the audience is able to understand it clearly.

The No. 1 cause for problems in relationships is misunderstanding. Misunderstandings occur because of miscommunication. This often happens when you ritualistically transmit your message and assume that the other person must have understood it. We could significantly boost our relationships at both home and work, if we learned the cat style of communication, rather than the monkey style of communication. An axiom of Neuro Linguistic Programming (NLP) is very insightful in this regard: 'The meaning of your communication is the response you get.' The efficiency of your communication is in bringing about the desired understanding or response in the other person. If the other person didn't arrive at the desired understanding or response, one should assume that there was some gap in one's communication. It is easy to give yourself a clean chit saying, 'I tried explaining but they aren't interested.' However, such self-serving excuses will not serve the purpose of communication. If you are really interested, you will explain in a way that they understand.

A story vividly demonstrates this concept. Once, a merchant was on his way from his village to the nearby city to sell multi-coloured hats. Tired on the way, he decided to take some rest under a tree. When he woke up after a while, he couldn't find any of his hats. On looking around, he found that the monkeys on the branches of the huge tree had taken them all. He was immediately filled with worry and sadness. In desperation, he begged and pleaded with the monkeys to return his hats. They didn't. He then started shouting at the monkeys to return his hats. They didn't. Then he hurled the choicest of curses at the monkeys and threw stones, but all to no avail. Even more fatigued than before, he again lied down under the tree. Suddenly, he had an epiphany. He stood up and removed his own hat from his head and pointing it to the monkeys, provoked them with repeated grinning and a frowning face. Having captured their attention, the merchant suddenly, in an animated act, threw his own hat to the ground. The monkeys followed suit; they threw from the branches all the hats they had gathered. The merchant immediately picked them up and put them in his own bag. Then quietly and speedily he left the place. He went to the city, made a good profit and returned home happily.

Initially, the merchant put the onus on the monkeys to understand his message and respond positively. But on failing repeatedly, he realised that the problem was not with the monkeys but with his communication style. Consequently, he took the onus of communication on himself and did what was needed for the monkeys to respond positively. This story is a sort of exaggeration. We are not implying here that people we deal with in our day-to-day life are monkeys who need to be spoon-fed. People around us are sentient and sensitive but sometimes we assume too much and don't do our part in making unambiguous and complete communication. If at all we have to assume anything, let's assume that the onus of ensuring clear communication rests on us completely.

Organise Dialogue

All the steps so far were stepping stones to bring us to the point where the actual conversation or dialogue can begin. Not all conversations will have the same format and structure. A management team meeting, a performance appraisal session, a feedback session, a public lecture, a training workshop, a conflict resolution dialogue—different types of meetings will have different formats and structures. Depending on factors like setting, medium, purpose, audience, etc., the conversation proceeds differently. Nonetheless, there are two principal components of any conversation or dialogue:

- Transmission: Verbal and Non-verbal Communication
- Reception: Active Listening

Transmission: Verbal and Non-verbal Communication

The way a message is delivered often affects the way it is received. Prof. Albert Mehrabian of the University of California in Los Angeles says that three elements contribute to the overall meaning of the message as perceived by the listener—words, tone and body language.[4] In fact, he assigned a percentage of influence which each factor has in the overall perception of the listener:

- Words account for 7%
- Tone of voice accounts for 38%
- Body language accounts for 55% of the message

The exact percentage contribution of each of these factors has been much debated since the research was released by Mehrabian in the 1970s. However, the study gives us the three main constituents of message transmission.

Words

Words have changed the face of the world. Following are some famous examples:

'I have a dream.'
—Martin Luther King Jr., *American Civil Rights Movement*

'Mr Gorbachev, tear down this wall.'
—Ronald Reagan, *Fall of Berlin Wall*

'Eppur si muove!' or **'And yet it moves.'**
—Galileo Galilei, *Heliocentric theory*

Someone has rightly said that words can act as windows or as walls. As windows, they can give others a clear view of our thoughts and feelings and facilitate understanding and relationship building. As walls, they can block others' vision of our perspective and cause misunderstandings and schisms in relationships. Choosing the right words is both an art and a science. As discussed in the beginning of this chapter, three primary characteristics of good speech as mentioned in the Bhagavad Gita are truthful *(satyam)*, pleasing *(priyam)* and beneficial *(hitam)*.

Regularly reading works of literature can enhance your command on words. You could read mind-expanding spiritual literature, biographical works and even good works of fiction to build up your linguistic repertoire.

Tone

People hear what you say but they decode it based on *how* you say it. The tone and emphasis with which the message is imparted can have great bearing on the meaning as understood by the listener. Please see how the meaning differs as the emphasis changes in the statement: 'You cannot crack that exam.'

> ***YOU*** cannot crack that exam.
> You ***CANNOT*** crack that exam.
> You cannot ***CRACK*** that exam.
> You cannot crack ***THAT*** exam.
> You cannot crack that ***EXAM***.

Body Language

An article on communication in *Forbes* states that whatever we're feeling in the subconscious mind first shows up in our body and only later (nanoseconds later) in our conscious minds.[5] So, if we're hungry, impatient or angry, our bodies pretty reliably signal those feelings to our audience. Neuroscientists have deciphered an inner mechanism within us which reads the emotions of others. There are mirror neurons in our brains that fire when our subconscious minds register an emotion in someone else, thus signaling to the conscious mind the feelings of the other person. While we are consciously trying to make our best pitch to communicate our message through speech, every other limb of our body is often, without our knowledge, acting like a radio transmitter, sending out the vibes which are playing within us through eye movements, facial expressions, hand gestures, energy levels, etc. If there is any incongruence between our verbal message and bodily expressions, it can be perceived by a discerning audience. It is therefore beneficial to have a dialogue with your subconscious mind and take it in confidence about the message you are going to relay—whether on a podium, in person or in a meeting. This inner dialogue will ensure that your body language is in sync with your verbal language and your message will be compelling and convincing. Following are some of the aspects of body language which have the power to leverage the effectiveness of your communication exponentially:

- S (Square): Face squarely, i.e. sit face to face, not diagonally. This reflects your involvement. Even if seated in a group, you can turn in some way toward the person to whom you are speaking. Directing one's body toward a person indicates, 'I am attentive to you.'
- E (Eye Contact): Maintain eye contact. It shall help you avoid distractions and bring vitality to the conversation.
- L (Lean): Leaning forward when a person is talking to you indicates that you are interested in listening to what they have to say. Don't sit very distant, else you will appear unreachable to the other person.

- E (Ease): It's important to be at ease and avoid fidgeting when a person is talking to show you are focused. Avoid making any time-urgent movements such as checking your watch or mobile repeatedly as it indicates that you are overly concerned about how much time has passed.
- R (Reciprocation): Observe and respond to the emotions and expressions of your counterpart. You could paraphrase and ask questions in between for clarification. You could respond with gestures and facial expressions like a nod or a smile or a frown. Gestures are movements made with body parts (example: hands, arms, fingers, head, legs). You could nod your head to indicate approval. Hand gestures could be made to emphasise a certain point. It is said that the face is the index of the mind. People read your face before they hear your words. No matter how dexterously you articulate your message, it won't have credibility if your face tells them a different story.

The verbal and non-verbal elements as mentioned above complement one another in making impactful communication. Lack of congruence in the verbal and non-verbal elements of your communication make your message unconvincing and leave your audience incredulous.

Reception: Active Listening

Listening, though apparently passive, is the most important limb of any kind of communication. If communication between two people or parties is compared to a bridge, speaking would represent one half of the bridge while listening would represent the other half. It doesn't take much common sense to figure out what would happen if half of the bridge is broken. Nothing and no one would be able to reach the other end. Rather, there may be an accident halfway through. Thus, many conversations meet an untimely demise because of this broken bridge.

If you find yourself talking most of the time in all your conversations without investing in listening or understanding the other person, you may be in for a lot of frustration. Very often, it is the people who tend to speak the most that end up feeling the least understood. Why is it so? It is a very subtle science. If I don't have the experience of listening to others and trying to understand them, I might not be able to perceive being listened to and understood by others when I am speaking because I don't even know what it looks like. Listening is a language in itself. If I can't speak a language, I won't be able to understand when others speak it to me. Just try to apply yourself to listening to others, even though every bit of your mind may be clamouring to speak and grab others' attention to your thoughts. Through practice, perseverance and patience it is possible to gradually arrive in the space where you are comfortable listening and not being the hyperactive hijacker of all conversations. Gradually, you will begin to enjoy listening and find that even without speaking much, you are able to communicate more effectively, and more importantly, win friends and not arguments.

God has given us two ears but only one mouth for a reason. Because listening is at least twice as hard as talking. Most people speak at the rate of 110 to 140 words a minute, but we think at seven times this rate. Therefore, it's easy to get carried away by our own thoughts and not listen or understand the meaning behind what others are saying. We tend to lend only a part of our attention to listening and that too intermittently while majority of our mind space is occupied by things like:

- Planning the day ahead
- Brooding over the past
- Formulating a response to what is being said
- Judging the person based on what they are saying

Active/Empathetic listening is a way of listening and responding to another person which is aimed at improving mutual understanding. Let us compare the feelings when you are not heard and when you are heard:

#	*Feelings when not heard*	*Feelings when heard*
1	Neglected	Valued
2	Ignored	Acknowledged
3	Avoided	Understood
4	Rejected	Accepted
5	Taken for granted	Cared for
6	Unworthy	Trusted
7	Belittled	Honoured
8	Discouraged	Encouraged
9	Demotivated	Inspired
10	Dejected	Satisfied
11	Embarrassed	Confident

The above table makes it clear that we would like to be in a space where we are heard and as a corollary, we should offer that space to others too. Following are some paradigms of an active listener:

- **Be non-critical, be empathetic:** Hear with the lens of empathy and not the lens of criticism and fault-finding.
- **Be non-judgmental, be objective:** Avoid coming to conclusions and passing judgments. Just try to objectively gather the facts as they are being presented.
- **Be non-defensive, be accommodative:** Avoid taking any personal offense and trying to offer a justification to defend yourself. Be

accommodative and accept the person and their feelings. Feelings aren't right or wrong. They are feelings.

- **Be non-fruitive, be dutiful:** Don't let your agenda overcast your mind so much that you become insensitive to the other person and start looking for ways to manipulate and manoeuver the conversation to fulfill your purpose. Let the conversation be driven by meaning and not agenda.
- **Be non-calculative, be present:** Try focusing on the conversation. Don't keep calculating your response while listening or plan your schedule for the rest of the day. Absorb their speech fully, wait until they have finished, then think over what has been said before you decide how to reply. Give yourself fully to the conversation.
- **Be non-fidgety, be patient:** Avoid making time-urgent movements like looking at your watch or mobile.

Open Up to Understand, Learn and Adjust

A dialogue is said to be a form of conversation where two parties, holding different individual standpoints, try to move closer to each other, through the process of discussion, to a commonly accepted space. Imagine a conversation where both parties are adamant to stay fixed in their standpoint without caring for or taking the effort to understand the merits of the other person's perspective. Such rigid standpoints will lead to a standoff or stalemate. Two monologues can never make a dialogue.

The Bhagavad Gita speaks of three different types of conversations: *Vada*, *Vitanda* and *Jalpa*. *Vada* is a conversation carried out fairly and is directed towards ascertainment of the truth without either of the parties having any prejudice towards forcing the establishment of a particular conclusion. *Vitanda* is quibbling, or merely destructive argument in which one tries to defeat the opponent by any means possible, but does nothing substantial to positively prove one's own thesis. *Jalpa* is an unfair argument in which various deceptive means are employed to fool the opposition. *Vitanda* and *Jalpa* are forms of argument in which winning, not necessarily determining the truth, is the main consideration.

American journalist and humourist of the 19th century, Robert Quillen, put it succinctly: 'Discussion is an exchange of knowledge; an argument an exchange of ignorance.' To participate in a fruitful dialogue, one needs to learn to balance confidence and self-doubt or to balance courage and consideration. We may have confidence in our viewpoint but if we don't carry a pinch of self-doubt we may end up becoming isolated, insulated and stagnated. When people enter a discussion with rigid and closed mindsets, the discussion becomes polarised. Rather than bringing the two sides together, such a discussion pulls them apart. Maturity entails that we see both the positive and negative aspects of our viewpoint, along with the positive and negative aspects of the contrary viewpoint. Understanding begins when we can openly:

- Acknowledge the potential downside to our pole or viewpoint
- Express appreciation for the positive aspects of the other pole or viewpoint

Irish playwright, Sir George Bernard Shaw says, 'The moment we want to believe something, we suddenly see all the arguments for it, and become blind to the arguments against it.' We need to approach a dialogue with an open mind which is ready to assertively present its understanding while being open to appreciate and learn new things. It is often not the conflict itself but how we handle it which leads to schisms in relationships and organisations.

Noted conflict consultant, David Angel, in an article for *Medium*, groups conversations into four types: debate, dialogue, discourse and diatribe.[6] The grouping is based on a conversation's direction of communication (one-way or two-way street) and its tone/purpose (competitive or cooperative). If you are in a one-way conversation, you are talking *at* someone, rather than *to* someone. If you are in a two-way conversation, participants are both listening and talking. In a competitive conversation, people are more concerned about their own perspective, whereas in a cooperative conversation, participants are interested in the perspective of everyone involved. Based on permutations of direction and purpose of communication, we arrive at four possibilities:

- **Debate** is a competitive, two-way conversation. The goal is to win an argument or convince someone, such as the other participant or third-party observers.
- **Dialogue** is a cooperative, two-way conversation. The goal is for participants to exchange information and build relationships with one another.
- **Discourse** is a cooperative, one-way conversation. The goal is to deliver information from the speaker/writer to the listeners/readers.
- **Diatribe** is a competitive, one-way conversation. The goal is to express emotions, browbeat those that disagree with you, and/or inspire those that share the same perspective.

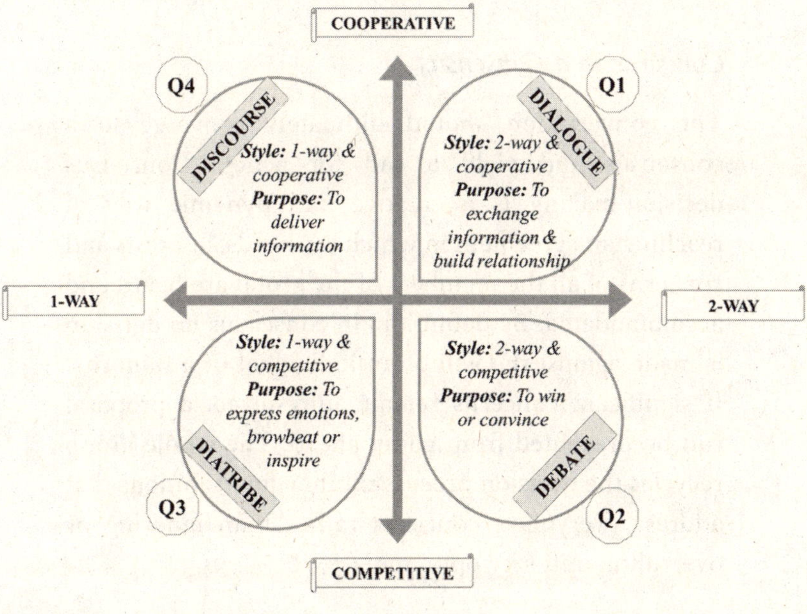

Engage Cooperatively

Good communication nurtures relationships. And what do people having good relationships do? Having aligned with each other, they support each other and engage cooperatively. Henry Ford once said, 'Coming together is the beginning; keeping together is progress; working together is success.' Coming together is about making a connection. Keeping together is about good communication. Working together is about creative cooperation. Here again we share three principles for engaging cooperatively:

- Converge to a Consensus
- Commit
- Collaborate

Converge to a Consensus

The conversation should ultimately converge to a consensus and yield a call for action. Consensus decision-making is a creative and dynamic way of reaching an agreement in which the needs, interests and concerns of all the members of the group are heard and accommodated. By definition, in consensus no decision is made against the will of an individual or a minority. If significant concerns remain unresolved, a proposal can be prevented from going ahead. The whole group recycles the decision process till they find solutions that address everyone's concerns rather than ignoring or overruling minority opinions.

An episode from the Mahabharat demonstrates how the process of building consensus can help resolve complex dilemmas. Ashvatthama had killed all the five sons of Draupadi treacherously when they were sleeping at night. Arjuna was furious. He rushed to Veda Vyasa's *ashrama*, where Ashvatthama was hiding. Assisted by Krishṇa, he overpowered the culprit. Soon, Draupadi arrived too. Arjuna asked her, 'As the mother of your five sons who were slain, tell me what punishment should I give to him? Shall I kill him?'

Draupadi wept as she thought of her children. But she said, 'I do not want Ashvatthama to be killed. He is the son of our Guru. I know the pain that a mother's heart feels when her children die. I do not want Ashvatthama's mother to undergo the same sorrow.' Yudhishtira, Nakula and Sahadeva supported Draupadi. However, Bhima angrily disagreed and recommended killing the aggressor who had murdered sleeping children for no purpose. Arjuna turned toward Krishna for a solution. Krishna told him that the arguments of Draupadi and Bhima were both valid and could not be disregarded. He suggested to Arjuna that he uphold Draupadi's sentiments and at the same time satisfy Bhima's. Understanding the deep import behind Krishna's equivocal advice, Arjuna struck off the divine gem that was embedded on Ashvatthama's forehead, thus disgracing him. Such disgrace is worse than death for a warrior. Arjuna understood that collegial decision-making is not about *one or the other* but about *one and the other*.

Commit

Without commitment to the agreement made in a discussion, the whole endeavour would be futile. All parties should commit to honouring the conclusions of the discussions and abide by the call for action. It is advantageous to set terms of accountability for the participants in order to ensure that the commitments are visibly delivered upon by all. In the absence of visible commitment from some of the participants, others may get discouraged and eventually back out, leading to a crumbling of the consensus.

Collaborate

Furthermore, the parties involved should keep cooperating and communicating with each other as the need arises. In Bhutanese folklore, there is a beautiful story about the journey from conflict to cooperation of four animals.

In a forest lived four animals—an elephant, a monkey, a peacock and a rabbit. In the beginning, they were not friends. They argued about who had the right to a fruit tree, whose delicious fruit was enjoyed by all of them. Each of the animals staked claims to the fruit tree and overruled the others. The monkey claimed the fruits on account of the tree being his natural habitat. The peacock claimed that the fruits hung in the sky and so they belonged to the birds. The rabbit countered them by saying that the rabbits and trees are natural friends because both take shelter in soil and so rabbits have right to the fruits first. Meanwhile, the elephant threatened others saying that he is the most powerful of all and so deserves to be obeyed by them. This argument stopped when a woodcutter arrived on the scene and cut the tree down. The four animals realized that they needed each other's help to regain the fruit they all loved. They wanted to help each other so they became friends. They decided that rather than using their strengths against each other, they will derive from each other's strength to attain their common goal. Thus, a cooperative conversation ensued:

'I will plant a seed in the ground,' the peacock said.

'I will water it,' the monkey said.

'I will fertilise the soil,' said the rabbit.

'I will protect it,' said the elephant.

The seed grew and grew until it became a tree. Then came the lovely fruits. Through their friendship and cooperation, the four were able to share their favourite fruit. We see that the four friends were able to arrive at a call for action, commit to it and finally collaborate with each other to attain their common goal.

The process of communication as discussed has been summed up in the diagram on the following page:

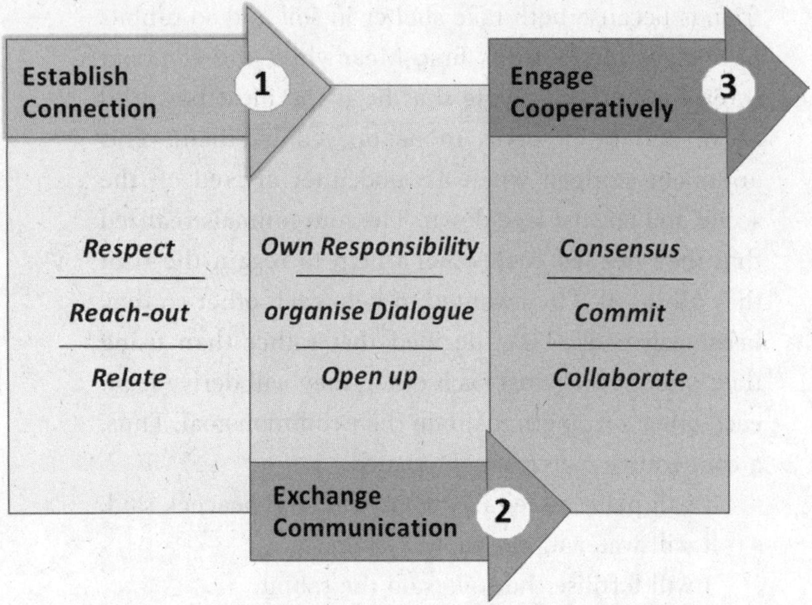

3-Step Communication Process

Soundless Communication

No communication is also an important form of communication. Knowing when not to communicate is also as important as learning to communicate effectively. Sometimes silence is the best communication strategy. It is important to understand that we need not give justification or rationale behind our decisions to everyone. If key stakeholders are in consensus and are convinced about the vision, they should begin the journey. Many people may not be able to immediately see the merit of your decision—time and results will speak for the vision eventually. A thought-provoking story from the Panchatantra demonstrates this principle.

Once upon a time, next to a lake, there lived a tortoise and two geese who were great friends. As the lake was drying, the geese decided to migrate to a new place. They wanted to take the tortoise with them but didn't know how to do so. The tortoise couldn't fly like them but he came up with a brilliant idea. He asked the geese to hold the ends of a stick with their beaks while he would hold it from the middle with his mouth. The geese were impressed by the tortoise's sharp intellect but they suggested that the tortoise should not open his mouth during the journey and let go of the stick. As per the plan, the geese clamped up the stick in their beaks, with the tortoise grabbing on to it in the middle and the flight took off. As they flew high, some onlookers were amused by the peculiar scene and started commenting that the tortoise was dull-headed and was being kidnapped by the smart geese. They exclaimed: 'Oh, the poor tortoise!' This angered the tortoise and he felt that being the owner of the idea, it was his responsibility to explain his brilliant idea to those dimwits. He immediately opened his mouth to share his wisdom. As soon as he did, he fell to the ground and died.

Moral of the Story: Don't get affected or dejected by remarks or the dissonance of onlookers. You need not justify everything that you do to everyone. Sometimes silence is the best way you can communicate.

COMMUNICATION SKILLS: ACTIVITY 1

Chinese Whispers

This is a very old game which can help us understand how communication can turn into miscommunication innocuously.

In a group, call one person and whisper a word in their ear.

They have to go back and whisper the same word, only once, into the ear of the person seated next to them.

This will continue till the last participant has heard the word.

This participant will announce the word aloud to the class.

Is this the same word which you had originally whispered?

COMMUNICATION SKILLS: ACTIVITY 2

Communication Planner

This is a form which shall help you design a communication process so that you can have meaningful and effective communication with an audience of your choice. The form consists of a series of questions which sequentially take you through the process of communication as discussed in this section. Think of an audience or a person with whom you want to have important communication and fill in answers to the following questions.

Name of the person or group with whom you want to communicate:

____

What do you want to communicate to them:

ESTABLISHING CONNECTION

Respect

Respect is like the circuit breaker in a relationship. Disrespect disconnects us. It causes the connection to trip. If you cannot respect, you cannot connect and consequently cannot communicate. When people perceive disrespect, they retract and insulate themselves from any further contact.

What are the current respect levels in the relationship from both sides? Is there any gap in the respect expected and respect delivered on either side? What steps could you take to enhance the respect levels?

#	*Mutual respect*	*Rating (1 to 5)*	*Steps to enhance respect levels*
1	Your respect for them		
2	Their respect for you		

Reach Out

In order to connect, you need to reach out to where the object of your communication is. Enter the physical, social or digital space where they are located. You cannot expect to connect to people while being cocooned in your own shell.

What is it that is keeping you distant or disconnected from the person you want to communicate with? Do you have a footing in the physical, social, ideological or digital space where your audience exists? If not, what could you do to reach out?

Relate

The most important aspect of establishing a connection is the ability to relate with your audience. You need to talk to them in their language—both literally and figuratively. In order for people to relate to you, they should find your message to be relevant to them. You need to step into their shoes, understand their perspectives and address their needs, interests and concerns.

Identify the needs, interests and concerns of your audience. How could you become relevant and relatable for your audience? What should be your language?

Their perspective on the issue:			
Which part of their perspective matches with yours and which doesn't:			
Needs	1.	How can you meet their needs?	1.
	2.		2.
	3.		3.
Interests	1.	How can you cater to their interests?	1.
	2.		2.
	3.		3.
Concerns	1.	How can you address their concerns?	1.
	2.		2.
	3.		3.

EXCHANGING COMMUNICATION

Own Responsibility

One very important principle of communication is owning responsibility for communication. The No. 1 cause for problems in relationships is misunderstanding. Misunderstandings occur when you mechanically transmit your message and assume that the other person must have understood.

What is the central theme or message which you want to communicate? What could be the inhibitions/fears/reservations/assumptions of your audience which could lead to your message being misunderstood or ignored? What additional information could you give or background work could you do for them to take your message as it is meant to be taken?

Open Up to Understand, Learn and Adjust

A dialogue is said to be a form of conversation where two parties having different individual standpoints try to move closer to each other, in the process of discussion, to a commonly accepted space. Two monologues can never make a dialogue.

What are the bipolar ideologies or differences of opinion involved in the dialogue? List down the pros and cons of both the polarities. How can the opposing ideologies be reconciled?

Organise Dialogue

Different conversations will have the different formats and structures. A management team meeting, a performance appraisal session, a feedback session, a public lecture, a training workshop, a conflict resolution dialogue—different meeting types will have different formats and structures. However, there are two principal components of any conversation or dialogue:

- *Transmission: verbal and non-verbal communication (message, tone and body language)*
- *Reception: active listening*

What is the message which you want to deliver? What is the response which you are expecting? Refine your message by passing it through the following filters:

- **Is it truthful?** (Correct, Consistent, Complementary)
- **Is it pleasing?** (Cordial, Concise, Clear, Contextual)
- **Is it beneficial?** (Constructive, Cause-driven)

What should be the tone, emphasis and body language while you are engaged in the conversation?

Engaging Cooperatively

Converge to a Call for Action

The conversation should ultimately converge to a consensus, resulting in a call for action.

Did the discussion arrive at a mutually accepted conclusion? What differences have been resolved? What is the shared understanding? How are the two parties going to navigate the unresolved differences? Note down the conclusion of the conversation in terms of the decisions and action items.

Commit

Without commitment to the agreement made in the discussion, the whole endeavour would be futile. All parties should commit to honouring the conclusions of the discussions and abide by the call for action.

What are the commitments from both sides? How will they be held accountable? What methods or instruments could be used to ensure accountability (eg. weekly reporting)?

Collaborate

Furthermore, the parties involved should cooperatively work together and keep communicating with each other as the need arises.

What would be the various modes and methods of communication between the two sides in the future? Set up a schedule for future communications including meetings, emails, etc.

3. TEAM BUILDING

Teem in Life with Teamwork

It is said that if you need to travel fast, go alone, but if you need to travel for a long, arduous journey ahead, get some good company. There are several situations where we need to co-exist and co-operate with others. In the 'Virata Parva' in Mahabharat, Vidura gives a list of things which one should not do alone: 'Do not eat tasty food alone, do not take decisions on important matters alone and do not go for a long journey alone.' In other words, the experience and efficiency of doing certain things is enhanced by doing them with a team.

Michael Jordan, one of the legendary basketball champions of the USA, did something that will be etched in history as a hallmark of teamwork. He was in a game with seconds left till the end, in a position where he could easily throw the ball, and if he made that score, he would have established a world record in the history of basketball for making maximum points in a game. Everybody was excited because he was so close, he could make that point. With seconds to go, to everyone's great surprise, he passed the ball to one of his teammates who was closer to the basket and that player made the point, winning them the game. The newspapers asked him, 'Why did you do that? You could have gone down in history.' He said, 'I am not concerned with that. When I'm playing, I'm only concerned with the team. If you want a strong team, every team player has to think in terms of the team first and one's individual interests last; otherwise, the team cannot be a champion team. Talent wins games but teamwork wins championships.' He added, 'That other teammate, even though it was an easy shot for me, it was an easier shot for him, so by giving it to him, we would have had more of a chance of winning the game. That is more important than me going down in history.' That is why that team won almost every championship in that decade. That is the strength of unity. Michael Jordan sums it up in his own words: 'Talent wins games but teamwork wins championships.'

Kalzenbach et al, in the famous book *Wisdom of Teams*, give a precise definition of team: 'A team is a number of people with complementary skills who are committed to a common purpose, performance goals and approach for which they hold themselves mutually accountable.'[7]

In Other Words, a Team Is:

A group of people working together in a synergistic way to achieve a common goal or mission. Team members share responsibility, hold themselves accountable for attaining the desired result and are prepared to sacrifice personal views to accomplish their goals.

A Team Isn't:

Just a group of people who happen to be working in the same room or organisation. Commitment and collaboration towards a common goal defines a team. Otherwise, it is simply a social gathering or club, not a team.

ADVANTAGES OF A TEAM

Teamwork, simply stated, is less 'me' and more 'we'. When 'I' is replaced by 'We' even 'Illness' becomes 'Wellness'. Therefore, we need to team up to teem in life. Teamwork when properly done yields the following advantages:

- Creates opportunities for more people to contribute
- Distributes responsibilities/workload
- Capitalises on varied skill sets/intellect
- Broadens perspectives
- Provides opportunities for development
- Generates more output
- Reduces risks

LEVELS OF TEAMWORK

The animal kingdom is replete with examples of teamwork at all levels ranging from co-oppression to co-operation. Let us look at a few examples to grasp the ethos of team work.

Teamwork of Crabs (Co-oppression)

When crabs are trapped in a barrel or basket, you need not put a lid at the top to prevent them from escaping. They themselves won't allow each other to get out of the trap. As a crab tries to climb out of the bucket, other crabs enthusiastically pull him down. This makes sure that no matter how hard any of them work, none of them make it out. While any crab could easily escape, its efforts are undermined by others, ensuring the group's collective demise. This phenomenon is characterised by the mentality, 'If I can't have it, neither can you.' Therefore, I have called it co-oppression, where the members of the team work hard to oppress and suppress each other.

Teamwork of Monkeys (Co-opportunism)

The teamwork of monkeys is quite interesting and a treat to watch. Though monkeys stay together in groups, they are not always on great terms with each other. Often, they can be seen gnarling and threatening each other. Their teamwork is often inspired by opportunism. In the night and early morning, especially in winters, they can be found huddled around each other in groups, as if they are very intimate. But as the sun starts shining and they no longer need the warmth from each other, they can be seen scaring and fighting each other over pieces of food. Monkeys are often infested with lice and they depend upon each other for picking them out.

While one gets freed of the bites of lice, the other gets to eat lice and vice versa. Thus, the teamwork of monkeys is characterised by opportunistic behaviour.

Teamwork of Geese (Co-operation)

Frequently in the fall, scores of Canadian geese fly long distance to natural ponds. What is distinctive about these flights is that the geese always fly in a V pattern. The reason for this pattern is that the flapping wings of the geese in front create an up-draft for the geese that follow. This V pattern increases the range of the geese collectively by 71% compared to flying alone. On long flights, after the lead goose has flown at the front of the V for a while, it drops back to take its place in the V where flying is easier. Another goose then takes over the lead position, where the flying is most strenuous. If a goose begins to fly out of formation, it is not long before it returns to the V because of the resistance it experiences when not supported by the other geese's wings flapping. Another noticeable feature of these geese is the loud honking. Canadian geese never fly quietly. The reason for the honking in the rear of the formation is to encourage the lead goose. The leader doesn't honk—just those who are supporting and urging the leader on do. If a goose is shot, becomes ill or falls out of formation, two geese break ranks and follow the wounded or ill goose to the ground. There they remain, nurturing their companion, until it is either well enough to return to the flock or dies.

HEALTH CHECK FOR A TEAM

In today's competitive world, minimising the margin of error is essential for survival and growth. While the margin of error from machines may have gone down to nano-decimals, the same doesn't hold true for human errors. Teamwork can have a cumulative effect on human errors—they can be drastically reduced or multiplied, depending on the wellness of the team. A Boeing study indicated that 65% of all airliner accidents between 1959 to 1986 could be attributed to human error.[8] Specifically, there were several instances of mishaps caused due to poor teamwork in the cockpit.

Consider this: onboard an Eastern Air Lines flight in 1972, while all three pilots became deeply engrossed in investigating a malfunctioning landing-gear indicator, nobody noticed that the autopilot had been inadvertently disengaged. Due to this glaring oversight, the aircraft began its gradual descent and eventually crashed. The situation could have been avoided had the captain delegated flight control to one of his co-pilots. In another instance, in 1978, while the pilots of a United Airlines flight were busy investigating a problem with the landing gear, the aircraft ran out of fuel after an hour of circling and crashed six miles from the airport. As it turns out, both the First and Second Officers were aware of the grim fuel situation but did not directly challenge the captain, who was preoccupied with the landing gear. Thus, a synergistic team is not a luxury but an utmost necessity. Without synergy, even the best of experts put together could end up producing retrograde performances.

A team is like a living organism. You can diagnose the health of the team based on certain parameters. Let us first begin with a health check to understand where our team stands as of today. You may ask yourself these questions:

- Are your goals shared?
    - If you ask all the members what the team's goals are, will they all give you the same answer?
- Are the roles in your team clearly understood?
    - Does everyone know what is expected of them and how that contributes to the whole?
- Do the members see themselves as a team?
    - Do they all know each other?
- Are the members all talking to each other?
    - And just as important, are they listening?
- Is the work getting done?
    - Is it being done on time and is it of the required quality?
- If someone is ill or away, does the gap remain unfilled?
    - Or can another member step up when needed?
- Does the team have the resources it needs?
    - This includes managerial support as well as financing and other practical resources.

- Does the team have efficient processes to solve problems and take decisions?
  - This includes having effective team meetings and being able to implement the most efficient ways of working.

The checklist above is a barometer for the health of the team. Now let us have a look at the various stages a team goes through in course of its evolution.

CONSTITUENTS OF A HIGH-PERFORMANCE TEAM

When a team is working well together, it will prove that the whole can be greater than the sum of its parts. The idea is that in a cohesive group, the overall output is more than the total output of its members working individually. The group, as a whole, outperforms even its best individual members working separately, even if they are working towards the same goal. This is synergy at work. Team members encourage, support and inspire each other to rise higher in their individual and collective performance. It's not just about pooling different skills or combining strengths—it also has to do with the way the team members interact with each other. The total output may be lower if a team is not composed properly, is not in synergy or has insufficient resources or leadership because then it becomes easier for people to slack off under the cover of a team.

Teamwork was one of the key reasons behind the victory of the Pandavas over the Kauravas, who commanded a bigger, more superior and more equipped army, in the battle of Kurukshetra. One stark difference between the Kauravas and the Pandavas was that the Kaurava army was an assembly of powerful individuals while the Pandava army was a powerful team of cohesive individuals. All the great generals among the Kauravas, including Bhishma, Drona, Karna crusaded as individuals on the battlefield. However, the Pandavas weaved one team that was directed towards a single goal. As a result, the seven phalanxes of the Pandava army defeated the superior eleven phalanxes of the Kaurava army.

How do we bootstrap a high-performance team? Let us look into the five factors which contribute to creating optimum performance teams:

1. **Compass:** clarity and consensus on goals and roles
2. **Comradeship**: paradigm of interdependence or win-win mindset
3. **Communication:** ethos and styles of communication
4. **Composition:** synergy of diverse talents and personality types
5. **Captaincy:** good leadership

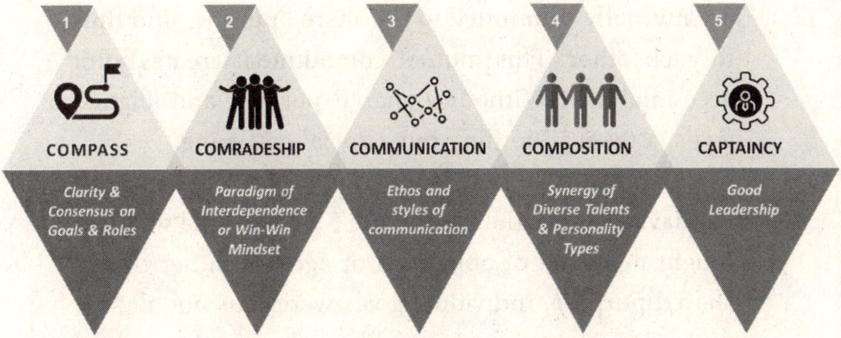

Compass: Clarity and Consensus on Goals and Roles

A shared purpose is the compass which gives direction to the team. Clear goals aligned with the purpose serve as milestones to fast-track the progress and monitor it. Additionally, when team members have clearly defined roles, each member serves as a piece of the jigsaw puzzle fitting together perfectly to create the big picture of shared purpose. Clear roles and goals comprise the proper superstructure of the team. Goals define what needs to be done and roles define who will do it.

Commitment to Shared Purpose and Aligned Goals

A team is a set of individuals who are bound together with a shared purpose. The collective goals of the team as well as the goals of the individuals should be aligned to this shared purpose. The shared purpose is born out of the vision and mission of the organisation and should create a sense of doing something important together amongst the members. Members of the team are mutually committed to the shared purpose and thus to each other. This mutual commitment creates joint accountability. Without a shared purpose and aligned goals, a team is nothing but a social gathering.

Alignment to the shared purpose helped the Pandavas win. In the case of the Kauravas, the warriors fought more out of obligation or agenda, rather than a shared purpose. Individual goals were thus not aligned to the team's purpose. Let us have a look at the goals of some of the Kaurava warriors:

- Bhishma
  - Fought to keep his vow to protect the throne of Hastinapur, not for the cause of Duryodhana.
  - Vowed to kill ten thousand soldiers each day but would refrain from killing the Pandavas.
- Drona
  - Fought because of obligation to the throne of Hastinapur, again not for the cause of Duryodhana.
  - Would capture the Pandavas, but not kill them.
- Shalya (Nakula and Sahadeva's maternal uncle)
  - Was tricked to fight on behalf of Duryodhana, against his wish.
  - Loved the Pandavas and covertly helped them by humiliating Karna.

- Karna (brother to the Pandavas)
    - Fought to prove his superiority over Arjuna.
    - Promised not to kill any of the other Pandavas except Arjuna.

Further, the Kaurava warriors were not flexible enough to adjust their priorities for the team's success:

- Bhishma
    - Gave away the secret of killing him to the Pandavas.
    - Did not face and fight Shikhandi because of his personal vow.
- Drona
    - Abandoned his weapons when he heard that his son had died.
- Karna
    - Did not kill Yudhishtira and Bhima when he got the chance.
    - Gave away his *kavacha* and *kundalas* before the war.
    - Fled several times from the war when he was hurt.
    - Didn't save Duhsasana when Bhima was killing him.
- Shalya
    - Kept insulting Karna while in battle.

However, in the case of the Pandavas, every individual strongly cherished a goal which was aligned to the team's purpose. Each warrior took on the challenge of defeating a mighty warrior from the Kaurava side:

- Shikhandi—Bhishma
- Dhrstadyumna—Drona
- Satayaki—Bhurisrava
- Arjuna—Karna, Jayadrtha
- Bhima—Duryodhana and all his brothers
- Sahadeva—Shakuni and his sons
- Nakula—Karna's sons

And they were ready to bend their individual priorities in favour of the team's success:

- Yudhishtira
    - Knew well that he couldn't stand against Karna in combat but still dueled with him to set an example.
    - Didn't hesitate to tell a lie about killing Ashvatthama, on Krishna's advice.
    - Yudhishtira and Arjuna resolved their internal conflict over killing Karna for the greater good of their mission.
- Arjuna
    - Killing of his Guru Drona by Dhrshtadyumna in a dishonourable way was very agonising for Arjuna but in the ultimate interest of the team, he didn't blow the issue out of proportions.
    - When Yudhishtira insulted Arjuna for not killing Karna and asked him to give up his Gandiva bow, Arjuna became impulsive

and wanted to retaliate. But on Krishna's conciliation, he calmed down.

- Krishna
  - Took up arms despite his vow to not do so.
- Abhimanyu
  - Entered the *chakravyuha* alone, staking his life and destroyed a big phalanx of the Kaurava army before succumbing to the unlawfully lethal attack of seven Kaurava generals.

Thus, when a team has a shared purpose and aligned goals, miracles become the new normal. Apart from being aligned to the shared purpose, what should be the characteristics of a good goal? In order to be effective, goals should also be **SMART:**

- Specific: Target a specific area where you want results.
- Measurable: Quantify an indicator of progress.
- Attainable: Neither out of reach nor below standard.
- Relevant: Goals that matter to your organisation/ unit and are relevant as per time, place and circumstances.
- Time-bound: Grounding goals within a time frame.

Specific: A specific goal has a much greater chance of being accomplished than a general goal. To set a specific goal you should be able to answer the six 'W' questions:

- What: What do I/we want to accomplish?
- Who: Who will be part of the execution?
- Where: Identify specific area/s in which you are looking for results.
- When: Establish a time frame.
- Which: Identify requirements and constraints.
- Why: Specific reasons, purposes or benefits of accomplishing the goal.

Measurable: Establish concrete criteria for measuring progress toward the attainment of each goal you set. When you measure your progress, you not only stay on track but also stay inspired knowing how much distance has been covered. Identify both lead and lag measures for your goal. Lag measures denote the results or output you are looking out for. Lead measures track the critical activities that drive or lead to the lag measure. They predict the success of the lag measure.

Attainable: A goal can be both high and achievable; you are the only one who can decide just how high your goal should be. But be sure that every goal represents substantial progress and yet is attainable within your team's means. A high goal might be sometimes easier to reach than a low one because a low goal exerts low motivational force. However, an unreasonably lofty goal might put the team in a mode of defense or complacency.

Relevant: Goals should be set keeping in mind the situation of the surroundings and the organisation or team. Conduct an environmental scan to assess the ground realities of the market you are operating in. Also conduct an organisational scan to analyse the capacity and strengths of your organisation or team.

Time-bound: A goal should be grounded within a time frame. Without a deadline there's no sense of urgency. If you want to double your sales and someone asks you, 'By when?', 'Someday,' is not a compelling answer. But if you anchor it within a time frame, 'By next year,' then you've set your unconscious mind into motion to begin working on the goal.

Defining Clear Roles and Responsibilities

Without clarity about their roles, team members are likely to waste energy protecting turf, rather than focusing on the task. Roles and responsibilities help people understand what they are supposed to do, where they fit in the bigger picture and who they report to, help avoid disputes and misunderstandings over authority.

Larry Bossidy explains in his book, *Execution,* that there is one job that no leader should ever delegate—ensuring that the right people are on the right job. It's absolutely critical that leaders fully understand the importance of having the right people in the right roles.

The role of a team member is determined by what is the best thing he can do in the interest of the team's goals, not necessarily what is the thing he is best at. For example, a team member who sports the cap of being an expert data analyst with a feather of being a good conversationalist may be required to use his feather more than the cap in some project, if that is what the team needs. This principle means that the interest of the organisation prevails over the interest of an individual; the interest of the family comes before that of one of its members and that the interest of the state must precede that of a citizen or a group of citizens. This principle is based on the understanding that in the long run, the individuals will benefit and flourish more if the team flourishes.

Mahabharata describes the division of roles and responsibilities of conducting one of the biggest religious undertakings held during the era of Pandavas—the *Rajasuya* sacrifice. During the Rajasuya sacrifice, King Yuddhishtira assigned different responsibilities to different individuals:

Yudhishtira Maharaj engaged all the members of the Kuru dynasty in taking charge of different departments for the management of the Rajasuya sacrifice. For example, Bhimasena was put in charge of the kitchen department, Duryodhana in charge of the treasury department, Sahadeva in charge of the reception department, Nakula in charge of the store department, and Arjuna was engaged in looking after the comforts of the elderly persons. The most astonishing feature was that Krishna, the Supreme Lord, took charge of washing the feet of all the guests. Queen Draupadi was in charge of the distribution of food, and because Karna was famous for charity, he was put in charge of the charity department. In this way, Satyaki, Vikarna, Hardikya, Vidura, Bhurisrava and Santardana, the son of Bahlika, were all engaged in different departments for managing the affairs of the Rajasuya sacrifice. They were all so bound in loving affection for King Yudhishtira that they simply wanted to please him.

Comradeship: Paradigm of Interdependence

In the team superstructure comprised of the goals and roles, comradeship serves the purpose of cement—it binds everything together. Comradeship entails sticking together through thick and thin and the willingness to make sacrifices for the unity of the whole. It is the attitude of placing *'We'* before *'I'*. This attitude of comradeship is born in an environment of trust. Relationships of trust thus act like the binder or cement which holds the team together. A lack of trust acts like a corrosive element which eats up the team from within. Lack of trust among team members leads to conflicts and suspicion whereas trust leads to cooperation and expansion.

Once again, a comparison of the Kaurava and Panadava armies highlights the trust and comradeship that made the Pandavas stand out:

- Duryodhana distrusted Bhishma and Drona, felt that they were partial towards the Pandavas and repeatedly accused them of not fighting to their full potential.

- Bhishma and Karna kept downplaying and insulting each other.
- Karna and Shalya despised each other.
- Bhishma and Shakuni had a strong mutual dislike. Karna and Shakuni also didn't get along well.
- Shalya and Bhishma too weren't on good terms with each other.

On the other hand, the Pandavas were a cohesive team—one team and one goal.

Everyone had great respect for their leaders—Krishna and Yudhishtira—and were united to fulfill their command. Apart from the leadership, the warriors had great respect for each other too. Furthermore, in the Pandava camp, decision making was inclusive as opposed to the Kaurava camp where decisions were passed top-down.

How can your team develop comradeship like the Pandavas? Comradeship operates on three principles:

1. Strength in Unity
2. Opportunities in Diversity
3. Win-Win Mindset

Strength in Unity

Aesop's Fables tells the story of a father who demonstrated to his children the strength of a bundle of sticks. When the father asked his children to break the bundle of sticks wrapped in a bag, none of them could do it. But, when they removed the sticks from the bag, and tried one by one, the sticks were easily broken. The father told the children, 'So this is the strength of unity. If we are bunched up, we can never be broken, but when divided, then we can become broken very easily.'

Another story from the Panchatantra demonstrates that when the house is not in order, outside parties can take advantage of the internal conflict.

One day two cats found a loaf of bread. Both the cats wanted the bread so they started fighting. They clawed at each other and fought for a long time.

Along came a monkey. 'Why are you two gentlemen fighting?' he questioned.

The cats snarled, 'We are fighting because both of us would like to eat the bread.'

The monkey asked, 'Why don't you share it?'

The cats said, 'We don't want the other to get more, so we are not able to share it.'

'All right,' said the monkey, 'I'll assist you to cut it in half.'

The monkey tore the loaf into two. 'One bit appears much bigger, let me get them to the same size,' he said, and ate a little of one of the pieces of bread. Then the other part looked bigger, and so he ate a bit of it.

The cats were so occupied fighting each other, they were not even aware of the monkey eating the bread. In the meantime, the monkey ate the entire loaf. The cats did not get any bread, simply because they were busy fighting.

When they saw the monkey running away, they regretted their foolishness and short-sightedness. The monkey had profited from their bickering.

Yudhishtira demonstrated the spirit of unity by offering his protection to the belligerent Duryodhana, when he was in deep trouble after quarrelling with a Gandharva. The Pandavas had a beautiful palace in Indraprastha along with incredible wealth and opulence. But Duryodhana siphoned away all their property through treacherous means and cast them into the forest for 12 years. To add insult to injury, Duryodhana wanted to go to the forest and flaunt his opulence and power just to humiliate them. But on the way, Duryodhana and his arrogant bandwagon were challenged and badly defeated by a powerful Gandharva. At that time, one of the men from Duryodhana's camp, came running to the Pandavas and said, 'Help us! Help us!'

Bhima retorted, 'Help them? Let them reap the results of their own sins,' but Yudhishtira said, 'No! We will go and we will fight for them. We will give our lives to fight to protect them.' Bhima said, 'Aaah! That man has cheated you and attempted to murder you! The man has humiliated Draupadi, and you want to fight for him?' Yudhishtira calmly said, 'We are all Kurus. The Kurus are now divided into the Pandavas and the Kauravas but ultimately we are all descendants of King Kuru.' He continued, 'When we are fighting amongst ourselves, there is a 100 of them and there are 5 of us, but when any outside force comes to attack any of us, then we should become a 105.'

In a high-performance team, the members look up to each other as links of the chain adding to the individual and collective strength, rather than perceiving others as threats, hurdles or bottlenecks. Such a vision helps the team stand up to any challenges or pressures inflicted on it by the environment.

Opportunities in Diversity

Diversity in a team is the bedrock for opportunities and innovation. People with different talents, natures and cultural backgrounds bring in different possibilities and perspectives to the team. But this diversity could be perceived as a threat by some of the members if it is not harnessed properly. The United States Marine Corps had to face the problem of harnessing diversity. In answer to this problem, they instituted a new training program titled 'Team Marine'. They developed a set of expectations defining what belonging to the Corps meant, one of which is: 'We expect to be valued as unique individuals.' By following this principle of seeing diversity as an asset, the Marine Corps managed to make what is one of the most diverse workforces in the world and unify it.

If there is a lack of diversity in a team the consequences could be:

- All members approach problems from the same angle.
- The team lacks fresh ideas.

- Or even worse, the team falls into the trap of 'groupthink' where it can envisage only one possible answer, which may well not be the best answer.

A diverse team will have a range of viewpoints and can potentially offer a greater variety of solutions to problems. But at the same time, diverse opinions can potentially create schisms and therefore, the next principle of win-win mindset is very important.

Win-Win Mindset

Teamwork doesn't mean that the members subdue and sacrifice their opinions and interests for the sake of appeasing others. Teamwork is about creative cooperation, where all the team members rationally and assertively present their needs and the team works towards creating a win-win solution for all. In the cat conflict story I shared before the consequences would have been much different if the cats had operated from a win-win mindset. Suppose the cats have grown wise after being cheated by the monkey. The next time such a conflict of interest arises they would deliberate and devise a fair means of distributing the bread—'You cut, I choose' rule. The cat which divides the bread now will cut it so that it is happy to have either of the pieces and hence has the incentive to be as fair as it can. This resolves the conflict of interest and eliminates scope for the opportunistic monkey to take advantage. Win-win mindset leads to win-win behaviour, which eventually produces win-win consequences. This is represented in the following diagram:

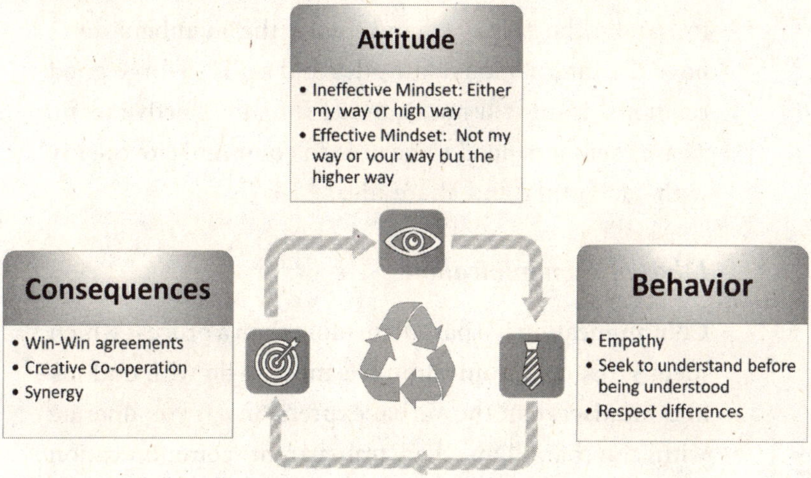

TEAM BUILDING: ACTIVITY 1

Interdependence and Gratitude

A team of two lists down the number of people they owe a thank you to in a 24-hour period. List all the favours received from these people (some known and some unknown). The team with the maximum points wins. The game helps each person count his blessings and understand the power of interdependence.

Communication: Ethos and Styles of Communication

Good communications lie at the heart of every successful team. A team may have all the technical skills needed to handle the tasks at hand, but if the members don't have the interpersonal attitudes and skills to forge good relationships it will not translate into an effective team. Team members need to be able to communicate openly with each other and share ideas.

Ethos of Communication

Communication is a paradigm more than a process which means that communication has more to do with outlook and mindset than the verbal expressions. If you operate with the paradigm that transparent communication is essential, other things will fall in place and your message will go through. Communication begins at the level of the mind, is articulated through our speech and is reflected in our body language and actions too. Most psychologists advocate that a major portion of the communication is transferred through the non-verbal medium which comprises of body language, tone, etc., whereas actual words spoken carry lesser weight.

TEAM BUILDING: ACTIVITY 2

Improving Communication: Back-to-Back Drawing

Divide your group into pairs and have each pair sit on the floor with their backs to each other. Give one person in each pair a picture and give the other person a pencil and paper.

Ask the people holding the pictures to give verbal instructions to their partners on how to draw the shape without actually telling the partners what the shape is. After they've finished, ask each pair to compare their original shape with the actual drawing and consider the following questions:

- How well did the first person describe the shape?
- How well did the second person interpret the instructions?
- Were there problems with both the sending and receiving parts of the communication process?

Code of Honour

Every team needs to agree to ground rules, or a 'code of honour'. Members need to know how they are supposed to work together and these standards of behaviour should arise from the team members' shared values. These ground rules govern such things as:

- How and when the team meets
- How members interact in meetings and in their daily work

- How the team interacts with the wider organisation

External factors may determine some of the rules, but the team can decide how to interpret and implement them. Going through the process of establishing the rules, over several sessions, will give members a better understanding of each other's values.

Even a team appearing to consist of 'the same sort of people' may have different core values. Failure to explore these and to build on them can lead to conflict and misunderstandings later. Furthermore, letting people know what is expected of them when they enter the team also makes for a smoother transition and better long-term relationships.

Another important part of having a 'code of honour' is 'calling the code'. That means that when a team member breaks a rule, it should be communicated to them in a non-intimidating but effective way. It may be mentioned very simply such as, 'We agreed that we would all be on time for meetings but you have been late three times.' Because everyone has agreed to the norms already, no further discussion should be necessary. If there is repeated breach of the code then further discussion with the transgressor might be required, or the group might need to talk about that item again and recommit to following it.

TEAM BUILDING: ACTIVITY 3

Creating a Code of Honour

A code of honour is a system for establishing and maintaining norms of behaviour within a team.

1. Ask each member to note down five things that they value most in being part of the team.
2. Share those values with the group.
3. Discuss them as a group. Allow all the team members to give their opinions Identify those that they agree with the most and then discuss how they would look if manifest in tangible behaviour.
4. Formulate a behavioural policy that reflects the value.

Here's an example:

VALUE: People should be respectful towards each other.

BEHAVIORAL POLICY: We agree that we will all come to meetings on time. We will respect and listen, without interruption, to the opinions of other members even if we do not agree with those opinions.

Continue until there is a list of about 10 norms that will guide the group's behaviour as they interact with each other. At the end of the session all members should read the list and agree to follow it.

Effective Team Meetings

Steve Jobs gave a simple formula for holding effective meetings:

- Keep meetings as small as possible.
- Make sure everyone is aware of the meeting agenda and someone in the team is responsible for each item in the agenda.
- Don't let people hide behind the PowerPoint presentations.

A detailed discussion on meeting management is given in a separate chapter.

Composition: Diverse Talents and Personality Types

In order to achieve the desired vision or purpose, people with varied talents and mindsets/personality types are required to accomplish different tasks. Good teams have complementary skill sets with some overlaps. Putting together a team is like solving a jigsaw puzzle in which you have redundant pieces too. You need to pick the right pieces, or else you may end up in confusion. Every correct piece has a place in the overall picture, if placed in its proper position. One thing to be noted is that each piece in the puzzle is unique and has a specific place where it belongs. It is the responsibility of the leader to pick the right people and place them in right positions for the optimal performance of the team.

Few people realise how important our individual personalities are to team functioning. The starting point of understanding people is to realise and accept the fact that everyone is not like you! There is a Vedic aphorism: *Atmavan manyate jagat.* It means that people see others with the lenses of their personality and expect others to fit within their spectrum. Different people perceive and respond differently to the same situation. Different is not bad, it's just different. One needs to broaden one's perspective of what is normal behaviour to be able to understand and accommodate different personality types which are needed for the success of a team. A helpful way to understand a basic difference in human behaviour is based on three foundational observations about normal behaviour:

1. Some people are **liberal**, while others are **conservative.** Some people are always eager to buy in or try newer ideas and ways of functioning. Others tend to be more cautious and reserved and are in favour of careful consideration before accepting any new change.
2. Some people are more **task-oriented**, while others are more **people-oriented**. Some people are focused on getting things done; others are more tuned in to the people around them and their feelings.
3. Some people are inspired by **creativity** while others by **execution**. There are people who

are good at coming up with ideas. They are valuable when the project is beginning and they will shed thoughtful and insightful light on a project during the planning stages. They love to come up with new ideas and solutions to problems, but their excitement and interest are in that initial creation. They are not so strong on attention to detail or the consistent application needed to get the job done. Others are more organised and like to see a job through to the end. They draw everything together, test and check and redo until the job is done right. They are typically willing to work according to a previously established plan.

All of these different personality traits are normal, though in contrast with each other. The presence of people with such contrasting traits helps to add versatility and vibrancy to the team. An optimal team needs a range of skills, qualities and personalities to accomplish its goals. The need for diversity should be kept in mind when:

- Recruiting a team from scratch
- Expanding the team or replacing a member

The Pandavas represent a diverse team with complementary skill sets and personality types. Yudhishthira, the eldest son of Pandu, was a man of truth and piety who attracted respect from friends and foes alike and was thus their natural leader. He was also a man of great control and wisdom, as was demonstrated in his answering of the questions of Yaksha. Bhima, on the other hand, was an impulsive and uncompromising personality. He was a fearless and brave fighter. His physical power was unparalleled and he was invincible in a duel. Arjuna, the third son, distinguished himself from all the other princes in his skill with arms, especially archery. Nakula, the fourth son, was a great swordsman and an expert at taming animals, especially horses. Sahadeva, the fifth one, was a mystic and a great astrologer. He was considered to be a wise advisor and an expert tactical planner. While Yudhishtira was thought-oriented and Bhima was action-oriented, Arjuna was a personality who balanced idealism and pragmatism. Nakula and Sahadev were more people-oriented. This diverse team was knit together and given direction by the love and leadership of Shri Krishna. All the five brothers brought different abilities and approaches to the table and thus formed a holistic combination for success.

Captaincy: Principles of Team Leadership

Good leadership is the pivot of a successful team. A team goes as far as its leader leads it and so a good leader at the helm is essential. The Panchatantra has an interesting story about how smart leadership by the king of a flock of doves helped them sail clear off a life-threatening situation:

Once a hunter, looking to catch birds in his net, spread some seeds in a forest grassland. A flock of doves was flying past that area that time. The king of these doves, Chitragriva, spotted the seeds from a distance and led his flock to feast on the seeds. Soon the hunter spread his net and trapped all of them. Chitragriva and his flock, however, kept their cool in the face of danger. He appealed to his friends not to panic for the elders had once said that they tide over dangers, who are not scared by crisis.

Chitragriva said, 'Let us fly together and land elsewhere where the hunter cannot reach us. We can then plan a strategy to get out of this net. If we don't fly now, we will be doomed.' Keeping trust in the strategy of their king, all the doves flew together. The hunter followed the flight of the doves and looking upwards chanted, 'They are flying together. But the moment there is a break in their unity they will crash to the ground.' When he lost sight of the birds, the hunter gave up and went home ruing the fact that he had lost his net too.

When he was sure that the hunter was not chasing them anymore, the king of the doves told his friends, 'The hunter has disappeared. Let us all now fly towards the city of Mahilaropyam where I have a friend Hiranyaka, who is a rat. He is our only hope. It is only a friend who will come to the aid of those in trouble.' The birds, heeding the advice of the king, flew to the fort of Hiranyaka in Mahilaropyam. Hiranyaka was happy to see Chitragriva with his retinue and asked what the matter was. 'All of us are trapped in this net because of our weakness for food. Come at once and free us from this trap,' urged Chitragriva. Hiranyaka said, 'It is rightly said that a bird can recognise food from fifty miles but cannot see the danger lurking next to him.'

After delivering this sermon, the rat set out to free Chitragriva first. But the king of doves pleaded with him to first liberate his friends. The rat was angry and reminded Chitragriva that it was fair that the king became free first and then the servants. 'No, it is not like that,' countered Chitragriva. 'They all have been loyally serving me and are dearer to me than life. I care for their safety first.' Pleased with his friend's love for his servants, Hiranyaka said, 'Friend, I know the duties of a king. I was only testing you. I will free everyone now.' With the help of his servants, the rat then bit off the entire net and all the doves came out. Hiranyaka saw Chitragriva and his flock off and went back into his fort.

A team leader plays several crucial roles which fuel the success of the team:

1. Visionary
2. Goal Setter
3. Coach
4. Meeting Convener
5. Resource Provider
6. Conflict Resolver
7. Personal Example

Visionary

Leadership requires various qualities and skills but the primary function of the leader is to set a vision and inspire the team to work towards that vision. The vision, and the team's commitment to it, is where a group's metamorphosis into a team begins. The good leader:

- has a clear vision of the future,
- communicates the vision to the team, and
- inspires people to commit to the vision.

Goal Setter

Based on the vision, the team needs to set clear objectives or goals. The vision needs to be broken down into key outcomes. The team leader facilitates a collaborative process to create the goals and ensures that everyone is aligned with these goals. The team leader also needs to ensure that the organisational goals percolate and are reflected in the subgoals assigned to each unit and individual in the team.

Coach

Good team leaders are good coaches to the team members. A coach is a friend, philosopher and guide who helps you to set the right goals for yourself, figure out how you can achieve them and motivate you to achieve them. The coach also helps you to discover your strengths and weaknesses and then helps you to sharpen the strengths and address the weaknesses. The role of the team leader or coach is to facilitate a team's thinking, to help them think more productively and effectively. However, it is the team doing the thinking, not the leader. As a leader you want to harness the team's collective thinking ability, rather than try to convince them of your ideas. The coach also motivates the team and helps them identify and realise their potential. Jambavanta acts as an ideal coach for Hanuman and helps him break free off his perceived limitations. He tells Hanuman, 'Oh, forthright monkey, you are the finest among all beings by the dint of your force, faculty, flair, and fortitude... why then is your unreadiness in this task of leaping ocean.... Oh, vanquisher Hanuman, you give a jump-start to leap the ocean. Indeed, you alone are the best one among all fly-jumpers, and this entire vanara army is anxious to witness your prowess. Arise, oh, lion-like monkey, leap over this vast ocean, oh, Hanuman, your escape velocity is indeed unlike that of all the other beings. Oh, Hanuman, all these monkeys are dispirited. Why this indolence of yours? You boldly triumph over the ocean as your speed is highest, supersonic, super-photic, super-cerebric is your celerity. As with Vishnu who trod the triad of worlds in a trice, you too triumph over...' Thus, Jambavanta persuaded Hanuman to get ready for action to leap across the ocean.

Meeting Convener

If not steered properly, the conversations in team meetings can go all over the place. So it is important to do a lot of placement at the beginning and throughout any meeting. Placement can cover how long the meeting will go on for, the goal of the meeting, everybody's role in the meeting, type of conversation that needs to happen (e.g. brainstorming, goal setting, etc.), any agreements made earlier about the meeting, follow-up items from previous meetings and so on.

Discussing problems requires less commitment than discussing solutions. A leader gently steers the team toward a more useful direction, such as focusing on solutions and then letting them do the thinking.

As the chairperson of the meeting, the leader would also need to clarify and summarise the discussion intermittently. This helps bring conclusions to a complex set of ideas by simplifying the conversation to the bottom line. This also helps raise the conversation to the next level.

Resource Mobiliser

Whenever there is a gap in the availability of resources in terms of manpower, skills, finances, raw materials, etc., and the team is not able to fill the gap, it is the responsibility of the team leader to arrange for the required resources so that the operations can seamlessly continue. Shri Rama demonstrates his acumen in resource allocation and mobilisation by assigning different divisions of his monkey army headed by different commanders to be positioned at specific gates of Ravana's Lanka. This is depicted in Chapter 24 of the *Yuddha Kanda* in the Ramayana. Later on, Shri Rama revises the resource allocation to the battalions based on the latest news brought to him by Vibhishana's spies as described in Chapter 37 of the *Yuddha Kanda*.

Conflict Resolver

A critical role of the team leader is to create synergy and comradeship in the team. However, despite all efforts at creating synergy, there could still be serious conflicts. At such times, it is the duty of the team leader to step in and help resolve the conflicts.

Personal Example

Krishna states in the Bhagavad Gita that the path tread by a leader becomes the roadmap for the people in general: *yad yad acarati srestha*. An ancient Indian wisdom text, *Vayu Purana*, gives the definition of a leader or an acharya as one who sets example by personal conduct:

acinoti yah shastrarthan
svacaraih sthapayaty api |
svayam acarate yasmat
tasmad acarya ucyate ||

Such a person is called an acarya or a leader who knows the principles of ideal conduct, behaves in that way himself, and inspires his followers to follow the same. Thus, he is an acarya.

In other words, the leader knows the way, goes the way and shows the way.

Before the battle of Kurukshetra, both the Pandavas and the Kauravas were canvassing to get support from various kingdoms. It so happened that both Arjuna and Duryodhana arrived simultaneously in Dwarka to ask for Krishna's support. Krishna gave them a choice; one of them could have his army, the fearsome Narayani Sena, and the other could have just him—unarmed and not fighting. Without batting an eyelid, Arjuna opted for the support of non-fighting Krishna. Duryodhana smiled, thinking he had got the better half of the deal—what use was one unarmed man in comparison to an army of skilled warriors? But Arjuna knew that even the best of talent and resources, such as the Narayani Sena, were useless without the strategic vision of a leader like Krishna. It transpired that the lone, unarmed Krishna, serving as Arjuna's charioteer, was all the Pandavas needed to win the war of Kurukshetra. Arjuna had chosen wisely. Thus, the role of a visionary leader can never be understated in the context of team building.

Stages in Team Building

Despite putting all the ingredients together, high-performance teams aren't born overnight. They have to be built and carefully nurtured through several stages of evolution. A team grows up just like a person. There is a generally accepted dynamic which consists of four stages that teams go through as they develop:

1. **Forming:** getting to know each other and getting organised
2. **Storming:** trying to resolve conflicting ideas
3. **Norming:** working towards agreed goals and methods
4. **Performing:** delivering extra value through close teamwork

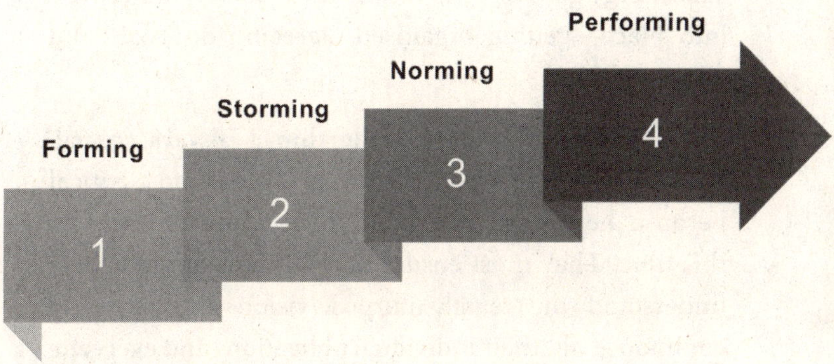

Psychologist Bruce Tuckman first came up with the phrase 'forming storming norming performing' in a paper written by him in 1965.[9] He used it to describe the path to high performance that most teams follow.

Not all teams reach the performing stage; some never get past storming. By looking more closely at these stages it will be easier to understand why this happens and how to avoid having your team breakdown somewhere on the road to high performance.

Forming

What it looks like: In the forming stage, people are trying to get to know one another, understand the team's objectives and see where they fit in. In newly formed teams, relationships are often cautious and noncommittal.

Not much actual work will be done at this stage. The energy goes toward putting the essential framework into place—getting organised, agreeing on goals and allocating tasks.

The leaders' role: Good leadership is always crucial, but during this first phase a leader's role is most critical because he or she will need to be quite directive at this time. They must ensure that all the team members understand the team's purpose/vision and agree to common goals, their individual obligations and everyone else's roles.

They also need to communicate when, where and why the team will be meeting. Offering opportunities for the team members to come together to build relationships will be very helpful at this stage. Team building exercises which might help people get to know each other could be conducted. As the team forms, people are still working largely as individuals.

The leader should take the opportunity to assess each member's strengths at this time.

Storming

What it looks like: The storming stage is marked by conflict and if the team is to be successful, then resolution of these conflicts is essential.

Most of the conflicts revolve around:

- **Goals:** Identifying the problems to be solved
- **Hierarchy and Roles:** Deciding how the group is to be organised and led
- **Working Styles:** Perceived threat due to conflicting ideologies/working styles/agendas

Typical storming behaviours include:

- Challenging authority
- Resisting opinions and improvements suggested by others
- Skeptical attitudes about the team and the project's success
- Arguments amongst team members even when they agree
- Politics/Formation of smaller teams
- Resistance to taking on tasks/Passing the buck

This stage can be productive if members are tolerant of each other and discuss ideas freely, keeping the focus on the team's real issues and overriding goals. If personalities get in the way of cooperation, or discussions get bogged down by minor details, the team may not move beyond the storming stage.

The leader's role: The leader would need to proactively help forge better interpersonal relationships in the team through group activities and his personal example. Also, leaders should try to be as inclusive as possible, or else certain sections may feel cornered. A critical component of the leader's role would be to effectively direct the meetings, guide debates and mediate the arguments so that members can participate freely and resolve their differences smoothly. The leader may also identify reluctant or unsuitable members and work out a settlement if needed. This is a good time for them to discuss the forming-storming-norming-performing concept with the team.

Norming

What it looks like: A norm is an accepted way of behaving or doing things in a group. If a team reaches the norming stage, it will have:

- Evolved its own working rules and protocols.
- Developed a sense of identity as a group.
- Have a single agreed goal (or set of goals), that all members work towards co-operatively.

In this stage, people know their roles and their places in the team and have developed working relationships with each other. Energies can now be focused on getting the work done. There still may be debates about the details of execution but the group is open and positive and ready to come to the table to resolve the differences in an amicable way. The members offer and accept constructive criticism without judgement or insecurity. There is clear and open communication instead of the red tape and distrust which were previously prominent. Development of trust is a key turning point for the team to reach this state.

The leader's role: The leader's role would be less directive and hands-on in this stage. They would take a more supervisory and supportive role. However, the leader would need to ensure that agreed upon ethics and protocols are being adhered to and in case of a breach, they may step in for course correction. Leaders should encourage taking initiative and offer opportunity for free expression.

Performing

What it looks like: At this stage the team functions as a closely-knit unit working towards shared goals with a strategic plan in place. Cohesion and synergy are the keywords which define the team at this stage. Leadership within the team is flexible and may shift among members depending on the problem. The team dynamic is characterised by the right balance of autonomy and interdependence. Members can act independently and make decisions, within stated terms and according to the criteria agreed upon by both members and the leader. While the members are at their peak performance in their individual areas of expertise, they complement and support each other. Redundancies and bottlenecks have been ironed out of the team by this stage and the team operates at optimal performance. The team can diagnose and solve its problems and implement necessary changes. It achieves its goals and strives to improve consistently.

The leader's role: Now it is mainly about facilitating and motivating. Some aspects of leadership will have been delegated to or assumed by team members. The leader should be on the lookout for identifying, developing and empowering future leaders at this stage.

4. ART OF DECISION MAKING

Apply the Head-Heart-Hand Approach to Decision Making

Life is all about moment-to-moment decision making. Consciously or unconsciously, we are making choices every moment. Advancement in technology has enabled almost everything in our lives to operate in an autopilot mode, without us having to make any conscious endeavours. Consequently, we find the same autopilot mode creeping into our decision-making faculty too. Cobwebs of prejudice and habits obscure our ability to make consciously and critically considered choices and we tend to go with the flow.

For a change, let us rise above the clutter and reflect on the journey of life. As we visualise a bird's eye view of our life's sojourn, we shall be able to see it as a series of decision-making events just as a journey can be mapped as a series of turns that one takes at various junctures. The turns we take determine our destination and our experience on the way. Famous leadership author and consultant, Stephen Covey says, 'I am not a product of my circumstances, I am a product of my decisions.'

Decision making has wide-ranging applications and far-reaching consequences. From routine domestic situations like choosing the menu for a meal to critical business situations like the bid for a tender, decision making is all-pervading. Lee Iacocca, former president of Ford and Chrysler, once said, 'The one word that makes a good manager is—decisiveness.' Is there a magic potion or wand to make our decision making foolproof? Can we at least make our decision making more organised and effective? No decision can be considered foolproof but we can make the process of decision making foolproof, organised and effective. This is what we will precisely attempt to do in this chapter. We will look at the disablers, the enablers and the process of decision making.

HISTORICAL DECISION-MAKING MOMENTS

Even seemingly small and inconsequential decisions have left indelible marks on the pages of history. Let's look at how certain decisions have impacted lives around the world throughout history. In the following passages we shall witness examples of some decisions which have had a great bearing on the lives of people for generations to come.[10]

Accepting the Trojan Horse

Legend has it that the Trojan War had been going on for a decade but the Greeks were unable to penetrate the walls of the city of Troy. Finally, they decided to engage in a little deception. The Greeks planned to trick the Trojans. They would leave a gift for the Trojans and pretend to retreat home. On orders from Odysseus, they built a horse, the Trojan Horse, which was big enough to fit a few dozen soldiers inside. After they wheeled it to the city gates, the Greeks faked their departure, and the Trojans, convinced they'd just won the war, rolled the gift inside their walls. That night, the hidden soldiers opened the gates to additional troops and the city of Troy was finally conquered by the Greeks. If only the Trojans hadn't decided to let their guard down and be more vigilant, they would have been able to thwart the Greeks.

Introducing Rabbits in Australia

Austin, a sheep farmer from England, had been asked to come and help establish the agriculture and livestock footing in Australia's Western District of Victoria. He built a retreat of nearly 30,000 acres called Barwon Park and introduced new animals and plants to the colony. Austin was fond of hunting and often hosted lavish shooting parties. But, unlike England, Australia had no animals in significant numbers to aim at. So, he planned to bring some rabbits from England and let them loose for breeding so that there would sufficient numbers for hunting. In 1859, he brought 24 wild rabbits on a consignment to Australia for breeding. Austin let a few go in hopes of hunting their offspring. What was thought to be a few rabbits, which could do little harm, turned out to be a menace. The rabbit population started expanding exponentially. By 1864, while Austin was still alive, complaints started coming in from farmers about crops being overrun and decimated by the rabbits. Although the jackrabbits certainly weren't native to the land, the land was perfect for them to thrive. In 1898, the population of rabbits was reported to be nearly 300 million. The human population in all of Australia at the time was 3 million.

Finally, in 1901, the idea of building a wall was raised and quickly approved by the colonial government. But a wall in a practical sense was a bit of an exaggeration. The fence would extend from new South Wales to Southern Australia, a distance of about 346 miles, effectively creating a border along the northern mid-territories. The fence's objective was to keep the rabbits from spreading into the western territories. Two more fences were built extending the length to nearly 1500 miles in total. However, even such a massive enterprise couldn't check the damage caused by the rabbits. Introducing rabbits in Australia had just meant a sport for Austin but it cost the government dearly. If the decision to introduce rabbits in Australia had been weighed in more prudently or the rabbits were introduced in a controlled manner, the situation could have been different.

The Titanic Loophole

The sinking of the Titanic is one of the greatest naval tragedies in history. More than a century ago, the RMS Titanic set sail on her maiden voyage across the North Atlantic. But just five days into the trip from England to

New York City, the luxury liner collided with an iceberg off the coast of Newfoundland; consumed by damage she sank, killing more than 1,500 passengers and crew. Multiple mistakes were made that collectively sent the Titanic to its tragic end in April 1912. First, there were no safety regulations in place for a ship as large as the Titanic. It didn't carry adequate safety equipment. For example, there were only 16 lifeboats, enough for only about one-third to half of the passengers on board, and crew members weren't prepared with binoculars or proper lighting. Additionally, the Titanic was untested. Though the ship's equipment had been tested, it was never test driven. The crew was not fully up to speed on the liner, its equipment (such as the state-of-the-art Marconi wireless messaging system) and its emergency procedures.

The ship, famously described as 'unsinkable', hit an iceberg in the Atlantic and sank shortly thereafter. A last-minute decision to switch officers proved to be another folly. On the night of 14 April 1912, the watchman assigned to the crow's nest post atop the Titanic had a problem. The binoculars he needed to keep an eye out for large obstacles (say, icebergs), were inside a locker—and the key was missing. Right before the ship left port, the cruise company made a last-minute decision to replace the ship's second officer, David Blair, with Charles Lightroller. In his haste to make the switch, Blair forgot to hand over the keys to the locker to Charles and thus locked the fate of the ship. The decisions to neglect going for a test drive or not keeping enough lifeboats or changing the second officer at the last moment caused the 'unsinkable' to sink.

Cool Nerves Prevented Cold War from Turning into a Nuclear War

Stanislav Petrov may not be a household name, but without him, there may not have been many households. The lieutenant for the Soviet Union Air Defense Forces was working an overnight shift in September 1983, when his computer showed that five U.S. missiles were heading toward his country. He could have immediately reported the missiles, which likely would have resulted in all-out nuclear war, but he didn't. Something wasn't right; why would the Americans only send five missiles? He checked the computer and confirmed it was a malfunction. NPR reports that this incident and the Cuban Missile Crisis are considered the closest instances of nuclear exchange between the U.S. and the Soviets—and the former was prevented by a single man trusting his gut and not making any panicked decisions.

Napoleon Invading Russia

In June 1812, Napoleon invaded Russia with one of the largest armies ever assembled for battle and was so confident of his impending victory he wagered the war wouldn't last more than 20 days. But due to lice infestations and subsequent typhus infections, food shortages, freezing temperatures and, eventually, fierce Russian troops, the Grande Armee didn't make it beyond Moscow.

More than 600,000 men from Napoleon's empire marched toward Russia, but just a few more than 100,000 were left fighting by early September 1812, and in the end, Napoleon was escorted by Russian troops back to France.

Decca Records Declining to Sign the Beatles

In 1962, Dick Rowe, an executive at Decca Records, thought that guitar groups were losing popularity. On New Year's Eve that year, The Beatles auditioned for Decca Records. Dick Rowe heard their audition a month later on a 12-inch audio tape and turned them down.

Dick Rowe was mistaken. The Beatles went on to sign with EMI and released their first eight albums through the Parlophone label. It's estimated that the band earned $38.5 million by the end of the summer of 1967. *The Wall Street Journal* estimated $50 million in record sales in the U.S. alone in 1964. In 1968 they launched their own record label, Apple Records.

Famous Electronic Brands Failing to Capture the Digital Market

The 21st century has seen the extinction of big, hallowed brands who weren't agile enough to keep up with technology. In the late 1990s and early 2000s, Nokia was the global leader in mobile phones. However, with the evolution of internet technology, it was evident that data, not voice, was the future of communication. But Nokia's reluctance to switch from their focus on hardware to software left it beaten down under by newer players like Samsung and iPhone, who understood the pulse of the market. Similarly, Kodak made the monumental blunder of clinging to analog cameras instead of moving quickly to digital. The company has the credit for being the first company to hold the patent for digital technology in 1975. However, it held back from developing digital cameras out of fear of eradicating its product lines for manufacturing consumables such as films, chemicals and paper which contributed to the company's profits. Competitors, such as the Japanese firm, Canon, grasped this opportunity and consequently outlived the giant. Kodak's inability to encash on its acquisition of a photo sharing site called Ofoto in 2001 also shows its lack of innovation. Instead of pioneering what might have been a predecessor of Instagram, Kodak used Ofoto to try to get more people to print digital images. Kodak filed for bankruptcy in 2012.

Mark Zuckerberg Turning Down Yahoo's Offer to Buy Facebook for $1 Billion

In 2006, Facebook was raising eyebrows in the social networking space. At that time, it was a college site with roughly 8 million users, in just 2 years. According to Peter Theil, who was an early investor in Facebook, the company was making $30 million in revenue but it was not profitable. Yahoo, Inc. came knocking and offered to buy Facebook for $1 billion dollars. Theil recalls reminding Zuckerberg that he owned 25% of the company and could do so much with the money. The 22-year-old Zuckerberg responded by saying, 'I don't know what I could do with the money. I'd just start another social networking site. I kind of like the one I already have.' With a decade of Facebook success behind, we can recognise Zuckerberg's decision as prescient (judging by 2016 levels, Yahoo undervalued Facebook by more than 300 times).

Apple Bringing Back Steve Jobs as Its CEO

Steve Jobs and his buddy Steve Wozniak launched Apple from his family's suburban garage in 1976. By 1981, Apple went public and cracked the Fortune 500. But Jobs was forced out of Apple in 1985 after a long power struggle with the company's board and its then-CEO, John Sculley. However, over time, the company started losing its cutting edge and consequently, sales plummeted. The company had lost $1.04 billion in the fiscal year of 1997. The same year, Apple brought Jobs back as its CEO who led the company to its greatest successes, from the iPod to the iPhone and the iPad. The board's decision to bring back Steve Jobs, after firing him a decade earlier, led to amazing product innovation and to the creation of one of the most valuable companies in the world.

DISABLERS IN DECISION MAKING

Having seen how certain small decisions have greatly impacted the world, let us try to investigate the dynamics of decision making so that we are better equipped to respond. In order to make our decision making fool-proof, we need to identify the pitfalls and disablers, both internal and external, which cause prejudice or negligence to set in. We have categorised these disablers of decision making under two heads,:

- **Internal**
  - Emotional Frailties
  - Rational Negligence
- **External**
  - People Pressures
  - Situational Complexities

Emotional Frailties

Emotions play a major role in decision making. We undergo a variety of emotions while making decisions: confusion, anxiety, attachment, uncertainty, urgency, nervousness, confidence, trust, etc. These emotions play a major role in influencing and shaping our decisions. Therefore, it is imperative to be aware of them so that we are not duped into taking a decision influenced by hidden emotions. Following are some of the emotional frailties which act as disablers in decision making:

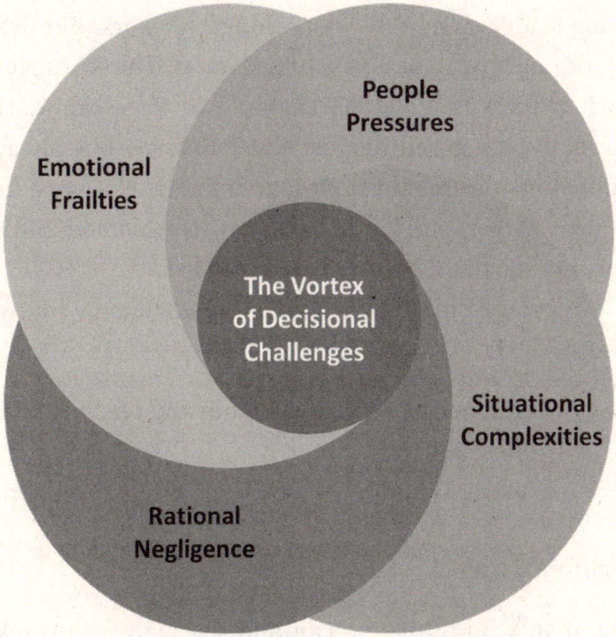

1. Escapist Mindset
2. Negativity Spiral
3. Short-Term Emotion
4. Psychological Blind Spots/Obsessions
5. Relativity Trap
6. Self-Righteousness
7. False Pride/Overconfidence Bias
8. Egocentrism

Escapist Mindset

Many a times the problem doesn't lie in one's ability to take decisions but in refusing the responsibility of taking a decision. We want things to work our way without us having to take a tough stand. The Kuru King Dhritarashtra is a perfect example of an escapist. He internally conspired against the Pandavas but always fulfilled his desires through Duryodhana. Not once did he take ownership for his choices. He blamed his ill luck, his sons and his previous misdeeds.

An escapist mindset is normally associated with two things:

1. Tendency to evade ownership and responsibility of decision making.
2. Shifting the onus on someone else's shoulder.

Negativity Spiral

'The man who thinks he can and the man who thinks he can't are both right,' said Henry Ford. Thoughts are like waves in an ocean. They keep building up as they reach the shore and their power is manifest only when they hit the shore. The thoughts we brew in the ocean of our mind build up as they reach the shore of decision making and that's when their power in influencing us becomes manifest. We are swept by the strong waves of our thoughts as we are carried away into making unwarranted decisions. 'Waking up early is not possible, I'm not used to it,', 'It's impossible to survive the competition.' How many 'nots' do we hear every now and then? This creates ample room for complacency and inefficiency to set in. Fear of failure is a major reason for the negativity spiral. 'What will people say?', 'What if I fail?', 'What if things don't work out?' In this way, we gradually make peace with mediocrity. This is known as the Dead-End Syndrome. Fear and insecurity then shape our decisions. In the Ramayana, there is an example of the monkey search party led by Angada being swallowed by the negativity spiral on not being able to find Sita so much so that they were on the verge of committing suicide.

J.K Rowling, the author of Harry Potter, is an example of a person who chose not to be swallowed by the negativity spiral. She was speaking to the graduating class of Harvard in June 2008. She didn't talk about success. She talked about failures, her own in particular. 'You might never fail on the scale I did,' Rowling told that privileged audience. 'But it is impossible to live without failing at something, unless you live so cautiously that you might as well not have lived at all—in which case, you fail by default.' The author didn't magically become richer than the Queen of England overnight. Penniless, recently divorced and raising a child on her own, she wrote the first Harry Potter book on an old manual typewriter. Twelve publishers rejected the manuscript! A year later she was given the green light by Barry Cunningham from Bloomsbury, who agreed to publish the book but insisted she get a day job because there was no money in children's books. But all through, J.K. Rowling consciously chose to be positive and not get sucked by the negativity spiral.

Short-Term Emotion

Cloudbursts are sudden, violent rainstorms that can suddenly flood and devastate a whole city. If you think cloudbursts are deadly, emotional cloudbursts are deadlier. Anger and frustration are some of the common emotions involved with emotional cloudbursts. Emotions and feelings bottled up for a while eventually lead to an outburst, manifesting as verbal or physical abuse and other such irreversible actions. Such emotional cloudbursts contain many unprocessed and raw emotions which can cause lifelong damage to our relationships and career. Taking hasty whimsical decisions when we are experiencing short-term emotions are risky. Such temporary emotions can have a permanent effect.

In the *Bhagavat Purana*, there is a story of Indra, the god of rains, becoming furious with the herdsmen of a small hamlet called Vrindavan for their decision to skip the annual worship they used to offer to him and instead expressing their gratitude to the Govardhan hill and the cows that were their direct source of livelihood. Although Indra was being worshiped elsewhere, this action of these simple herdsmen in a remote village irked him so much that he ordered clouds of universal devastation to inundate and destroy this small village. The legend has it that Shri Krishna, who is the Lord of all *devatas*, lifted the Govardhan hill as an umbrella and protected these simple herdsmen from the emotional cloudburst of Indra. Soon, Indra realised his mistake and fell on his knees to ask forgiveness from Shri Krishna.

Psychological Blind Spots/Obsessions

A blind spot is an area where a person's view is obstructed. A car's rear-view mirror has limited range and therefore you are faced with blind spots or areas which you can't see. We have certain psychological obsessions or attachments which act as blind spots, hindering our ability to see common sense facts. These blind spots are born out of attachment to a certain activity, object or person. Taking decisions on the basis of our obsessions is certainly unhealthy.

The Puranas relate to us the story of Sati who was rightly advised by Lord Shiva to refrain from visiting a social function which was being held by her father, Daksha. Daksha was envious of his son-in-law, Lord Shiva, and had even become inimical to his own daughter. In fact, he had ostracised Lord Shiva and humiliated him in public. Keeping this in mind, Lord Shiva didn't want to see Sati being insulted were she to visit her father's place. But, due to blinding attachment to her maternal family, she disregarded Shiva's advice. At the function, Daksha neglected her and disrespected Lord Shiva, which agonised Sati so much so that she set herself on fire.

Relativity Trap

Sharad was excited. After all, he was getting promoted to the post of manager, which also meant an increment. A pay hike of ₹15,000 made him feel like he was on top of the world. He was delighted until he got to know that Govind, his colleague got a pay hike of ₹20,000. Excitement turned into resentment, joy into jealousy, happiness into frustration.

How often do we measure our success or happiness by comparing how much others have? That one thing which seemed to be the ultimate elixir of happiness, on which we spent all of our time and energy, seems to become worthless in a moment due to the cancer of comparison. 'His house is bigger than mine,', 'Her car is better than mine,', etc. Here, greed overpowers need.

Two aspects of the Relativity Trap are:

1. Using comparison as the yardstick for righteousness and success: For you to be right someone else has to be wrong, for you to have more someone else should have less.
2. Using comparison as the yardstick for decision making: Making choices based on a statistical survey of what others are choosing.

The Mahabharata gives the example of Gandhari who hit her womb upon hearing that Kunti had given birth first, which meant that Kunti's son would become the crown prince and not hers. However, her choice of responding with envy meant that her sons were born with the same comparative mindset. All his life, Duryodhana measured his sense of self-worth by comparing himself to the Pandavas.

Self-Righteousness

The obsession with always being correct and righteous is an impediment to open objective decision making. Sometimes right decisions in life aren't arrived at by following the rule book to the letter. Along with the letter of the law, one needs to reflect on the spirit of the law to arrive at the right decision. While being chaste to the rules, one also needs to be compassionate to the people around.

In trying to be a holy and self-righteous person, Karna ended up being neither a loyal friend to Duryodhana nor a good brother or son. He neither fit in properly in the Kaurava camp nor accepted Krishna's invitation to join his brothers.

Overconfidence Bias/False Pride

'Overconfidence will drown you in
the sea of reality.'— Norain

The overconfidence bias is a well-established bias in the field of psychology in which a person's subjective confidence in his or her judgements is reliably greater than the objective accuracy of those judgements. Having an unrealistic estimate of one's abilities or a wishful self-assurance that one shall never fail acts as a deterrent to good decision making.

The *Bhagavat Purana* narrates the story of Jarasandha who attacked Mathura 17 times with an army of 5 million men which was wiped off every time by Krishna and

Balaram but it never occurred to him that his military strength was inferior to Krishna's unlimited powers. He always felt that the situation was probably not quite conducive or the strategy could have been better and thus kept attacking Mathura in vain and was crushed every single time.

Egocentrism

Sound decision making warrants that all factors involved in the scenario are given due weightage. But often it is seen that the decision maker gives excessive weightage to the protection of their personal interests, disregarding the interests of the institution and other parties involved. Such egocentrism on part of the decision maker or leader leads to neglect or minimisation of others' interests, keeping them on the periphery of decision making while keeping one's own selfish agenda in the center.

The Mahabharata narrates the story of when Krishna came as a peace messenger to Duryodhana and asked him to part with just five villages of his entire kingdom for the Pandavas. However, Duryodhana's ego didn't allow him to part with even that and thus put the entire Kuru clan on the verge of annihilation only to satisfy his ego. Duryodhana was so arrogant that he couldn't tolerate seeing anyone rise above him. In fact, he would not allow his servants to hold an umbrella over his head, even under the hot sun, because the umbrella would get a place above him. This sounds ridiculous but such thinking is not impossible for egocentric people.

Rational Negligence

Decision making requires due diligence. Scottish novelist, Sir Walter Scott, writes, 'I can give you a six-word formula of success: Think things through, then follow through.' One needs to think through to understand one's role and objectives of the decision under consideration and the various scenarios and risks involved. Following are some of the rational negligences which act as disablers in decision making:

1. Identity Crisis
2. Impulsive Decision Disorder
3. Paralysis by Analysis
4. De-valuation
5. Narrow/Short-Sightedness
6. Ambiguity of Purpose/Objectives
7. In-the-Box Thinking

Identity Crisis

One has various identities in life—that of a brother, a son, a leader, a father, a friend, a husband, etc., sometimes all at once. Mr Shyam Sen has a pharmaceutical business and has come across a prospect of making a profit of $1 million every year by compromising a bit on safety regulations for some medicines. He is in between two minds: whether to be an honest, upright gentleman whom his son can look up to, or a shrewd businessman who can mint money.

Vinay, a medical student, gets a call from his friends who want him to join for a weekend outing to nearby hill station. Vinay's exams are only a week away. He has to choose between being an agreeable friend and a sincere student.

In our lives too, we face situations where we are living multiple identities and are not able to ascertain which one to pick for making decisions. Arjuna was unable to choose between *Kshatriya Dharma* and his *Kula Dharma*, his duty as a statesman and his duty as a family man. What was his identity on the battlefield, a compassionate relative or a responsible warrior? Arjuna was contemplating quitting the war and retiring into the forests rather than fighting his vicious-minded brothers. His identity crisis was the reason for Lord Krishna to speak the Bhagavad Gita on the battlefield of Kurukshetra. We need to weigh our various identities in each situation and ascertain which identity or which hat takes the driver's seat.

Impulsive Decision Disorder

The fast-paced life of the 21st century makes us believe that we are playing a rapid fire round in life all the time and to be successful we need to fire right answers to all the situations even before life has fully revealed the question to us. Impulsive decision disorder is the tendency to choose or act in haste while minimising the importance of due diligence about the consequences of the decisions and actions. In addition to problems in relationships, impulsivity can lead to problems with physical health and finances, as well as legal issues.

A case study of impulsive decision disorder in the Mahabharat is that of Duryodhana who hastily induced Karna to release the Shakti weapon to kill Ghatotkacha, which Karna had reserved for Arjuna. As a result, Karna was less equipped to fight with Arjuna when they both met face to face, and ultimately was defeated by Arjuna.

Paralysis by Analysis

Paralysis by analysis is quite a contrast to impulsive decision disorder. This refers to a behavioural disorder where people perform endless analysis of the problem without any resolve to come to a conclusion and decision. A 2010 LexisNexis survey showed that, on average, employees spend more than half their workdays receiving and managing information rather than using it to do their jobs.[11] Though analysing every last option in the quest for the best choice may lead to an objectively better outcome in some situations, over-dependence on analysis leads to procrastination and inaction.

A classic case of paralysis by analysis can be found in the assembly of Hastinapur, where Draupadi was being disrobed in public. Great generals like Bhishma and Drona stood speechless and were unable to ascertain whether Yudhisthtira had any rights to bet Draupadi as a stake when he had betted and lost himself in the first place. Their paralysis by analysis led to injustice and irreligion.

De-Valuation

Values and principles are considered the yardstick or the True North for decision making. When you are sailing in the seas, you can navigate by looking at the compass or the pole star. Values are the compass or the pole star which help us ascertain which direction to go in and what decision to make. In a utilitarian society where everyone and everything is out for sale at a price, values like honesty, respect, compassion and gratitude don't have any customers. It is like sailing on and on in the Atlantic without any compass or direction.

Churning of the milk ocean (*Samudra Manthan*) is one of the most gripping tales of the tussles between the gods and the demons. The gods were united in their endeavours because they were driven by a common value system of service to the Supreme Lord and his creation. The demons on the other hand had the value system of opportunity for personal gain. Demons were all united in churning the milk ocean because they would have to collectively put in effort to gain nectar. However, once they snatched the nectar from the gods, infighting and quarrel started amongst them. There was intense rivalry to have all the nectar for oneself without having to share it with others. Thus, the lack of a value system leads to flimsy decisions and chaos in the society.

Narrow/Short-Sightedness

Decision making begins by first identifying the problem at hand. If the problem is not understood and defined properly, the solution certainly won't be effective. Two critical mistakes in problem definition are:

1. Narrow-sightedness: Narrow or shallow framing of the problem. One fails to understand the full proportions of the problem at hand and the root issues causing the problem.
2. Short-sightedness: Inability to visualise the distant future or linked implications. One fails to understand the future implications and linked factors.

Ambiguity of Purpose/Objectives

The decision on which product to purchase depends on what we want it for and what purpose it is going to serve. However, it is interesting that many a times our buying choices do not take into account the purpose for which the product is being bought. You start browsing the net to buy a kindle to read books but get overwhelmed with Black Friday deals and end up buying an iPad, which you never needed in the first place. Similarly, if we are not very clear and articulate about the purpose of our decision making, situations shall sweep us into making decisions which are far from the desired purposes or objectives.

Srimad Bhagavatam narrates the story of a classic conflict between Indra (King of Heavens) and Prthu (King of Earth). Prthu wanted to perform his 100th Ashvamedha sacrifice which was a universal record previously held only by Indra. Intimidated, Indra tried to thwart Prthu by employing sacrilegious means resulting in a war between the two. Brahmaji, acting as the arbiter, reminded Prthu that the purpose for which he was performing these sacrifices was world peace and to establish religious principles. However, this 100th sacrifice had now become more of an ego tussle while world peace and religious principles were going for a toss. Realising this, Prthu decided to settle with his 99 sacrifices, knowing well that his purposes were better served by not performing the 100th sacrifice.

In-the-Box Thinking

'In-the-box thinking' means:

- Inability to be creative and broad-minded
- Failing to develop a range of good, creative alternatives

Inside-the-box thinkers often have a penchant for taking the safe, beaten path and seldom invest time or effort into finding new or better ways to accomplish things.

An anecdote from the Mahabharat gives a case study of out-of-the-box thinking. At the close of the battle of Kurukshetra, Ashvatthama killed Draupadi's five sons while they were asleep. Arjuna defeated and arrested the terrorist and wanted to punish him. Bhima wanted a brutal death sentence for Ashvatthama. However, the soft-hearted Draupadi didn't want Ashvatthama's mother to suffer the pain of the death of her child which she was suffering and wanted forgiveness for him. On Krishna's indication, Arjuna thought out of the box and synthesised both of their wishes. Humiliating a warrior was considered worse than death for him. Arjuna gave a comic haricut to Ashvatthama and humiliated him by taking his crown and jewel off. Thus, he created a win-win solution for all parties.

Another story illustrates the power of out-of-the-box thinking:

Many hundreds of years ago in a small Italian town, a merchant had the misfortune of owing a large sum of money to the moneylender. The moneylender, who was old and ugly, fancied the merchant's beautiful daughter so he proposed a bargain. He said he would forgo the merchant's debt if he could marry the daughter. Both the merchant and his daughter were horrified by the proposal.

The moneylender told them that he would put a black pebble and a white pebble into an empty bag. The girl would then have to pick one pebble from the bag. If she picked the black pebble, she would become the moneylender's wife and her father's debt would be forgiven. If she picked the white pebble, she need not marry him and her father's debt would still be forgiven. But if she refused to pick a pebble, her father would be thrown into jail.

They were standing on a pebble strewn path in the merchant's garden. As they talked, the moneylender bent over to pick up two pebbles. As he picked them up, the sharp-eyed girl noticed that he had picked up two black pebbles and put them into the bag. He then asked the girl to pick her pebble from the bag.

What would you have done if you were the girl? If you had to advise her, what would you have told her? Careful analysis would produce three possibilities:

1. The girl should refuse to pick a pebble.
2. The girl should reveal that there are two black pebbles in the bag and expose the moneylender as a cheat.
3. The girl should pick a black pebble and sacrifice herself in order to save her father from his debt and imprisonment.

The above story is used with the hope that it will make us appreciate the difference between lateral and logical thinking. The girl put her hand into the bag and drew out a pebble. Without looking at it, she fumbled and let it fall onto the pebble-strewn path where it immediately became lost among all the other pebbles. 'Oh, how clumsy of me,' she said. 'But never mind, if you look into the bag for the one that is left, you will be able to tell which pebble I picked.' Since the other pebble is black, it must be assumed that she had picked the white one. And since the moneylender dared not admit his dishonesty, the girl changed what seemed to be an impossible situation into an advantageous one.

Most complex problems do have a solution; sometimes we just have to think about them in a different way.

DECISION MAKING: ACTIVITY 1

Internal Challenges in Decision Making—Emotional Vulnerabilities & Rational Negligence

Instructions for the exercise:

- Select a real-life complex decision situation at an individual, interpersonal or organisational level.
- Below is a list of challenges in decision making which one may encounter if one is not sufficiently watchful. Reflect on your case and ascertain which of the following pitfalls could one fall into while making decisions in such a situation.
- Write a summary of your findings.

Emotional Frailties

Emotional vulnerabilities	***Explanation***	***Possible instance of pitfall in reference to the Case Study provided***
Escapist mindset	• Tendency to evade ownership and responsibility of decision making • Putting the onus on someone else's shoulder	
Negativity spiral	• Dead-end syndrome: No solution exists • Emotions of insecurity and fear driving the decisions	
Short-term emotion	• Emotional cloudburst which may lead to whimsical decisions which are repented later	
Psychological blind spots/obsessions	• Attachments which cover or distort one's vision of the people, situation and the outcomes	

Emotional Vulnerabilities	*Explanation*	*Possible instance of pitfall in reference to the Case Study provided*
Relativity trap	• Using comparison as the yardstick for decision making • For you to be right someone else has to be wrong, for you to have more someone else should have less	
Self-righteousness	• Obsession with being righteous hampers one's judgement • Desire to project oneself as righteous and ethical	
False pride/ overconfidence bias	• Egoistic/Irrational belief in one's abilities and thus under-estimating the problem at hand	
Egocentrism	• Decisions dictated by one's selfish interests without any consideration for welfare or interests of others	

Rational Negligence

Rational negligence	*Explanation*	*Possible instance of pitfall in reference to the Case Study provided*
Identity crisis	• Inability to resolve conflicting identities and roles	
Impulsive decision disorder	• Hurrying/rushing either by habit or perceived time pressure	
Paralysis by analysis	• Endless analysis of the problem without resolve to come to a conclusion and decision • Procrastination	
De-valuation	• Not having any universal values and principles • Values and principles can be considered as the yardstick or the True North for decision making	

Rational negligence	*Explanation*	*Possible instance of pitfall in reference to the Case Study provided*
Narrow/ short-sightedness	• Narrow or shallow framing of the problem • Inability to visualise the distant future or linked implications	
Ambiguity of purpose/ objectives	• Jumping to solve the problem without pondering on the purpose or desired objectives	
In-the-box thinking	• Inability to be creative and broad minded • Failing to develop a range of good, creative alternatives	

People Pressures

Humans are social animals and so they don't operate in vacuum but amidst family, friends, colleagues and society. We do get influenced by their thoughts, desires, opinions, suggestions and sometimes threats. Thus, decisions aren't taken in isolation but in a charged environment of social exchange. Following are ways people pressures can influence our decision making:

1. Halo Effect/Relationship Bias
2. Coercion
3. Bad Counsel
4. Public Opinion
5. Activism
6. Groupthink
7. Failure of Consensus

Halo Effect/Relationship Bias

Halo effect refers to being influenced by the opinions or interests of a towering personality or a close relationship. When a towering, charismatic personality is around, it is tough to ascertain and stand by your own convictions. You tend to just get swept away by their charisma. A close relative or a loved one has a similar influence on our decision making. For example, people in general tend to get influenced by choices of celebrities. Because we find the celebrities attractive, successful and likable, we tend to also see them as intelligent, all-knowing and benevolent. This aspect of customer psychology is often leveraged by advertisers to promote products through these celebrities who might not be using the product themselves.

The episode of the churning of the milk ocean (*Samudra Manthan*) narrated in the *Srimad Bhagavatam* reaches its crescendo when Lord Dhanvantri appears with the pot of nectar. The nectar is promptly snatched away by the demons but they don't trust anyone amongst themselves to allocate the service of distributing it impartially. Just then, the Supreme Lord appears in the form of the most beautiful woman—Mohini Murti. The demons became so captivated by her beauty that they trust her blindly and give away the rights for distributing the nectar to her. She eventually deprives them of their share and distributes the nectar to the gods which goes on to show that making biased decisions under the influence of others' charisma may prove to be unpropitious.

Coercion

Coercion refers to being made to take a decision out of force or fear of some powerful person. We crumble under the pressure and are forced to decide against our will and reasoning.

Everyone in the Kingdom of Vidarbha, including the King Bhishmaka, wanted Rukmini to get married to Krishna but her powerful brother, Rukmi, wanted her to get married to Krishna's avowed enemy, Shishupala. Bhishmaka accepted this because of Rukmi's pressure.

Later however, on Rukmini's request, Krishna came, kidnapped and married her.

Bad Counsel

Advice and suggestions of others plays an important role in steering our opinions and decisions. Very often, we form our opinions by hearing some information or opinions from others, without verifying it properly. Sometimes, such advice may be fueled by selfish agenda or bias. As Socrates rightly advised, we must apply the three-filter test to what we hear about someone before accepting it:

1. Is it true? If not, do not care to listen.
2. Is it good or bad about the person? If it's bad, don't bother to hear unless you can bring about a change.
3. Is it useful for me? If not, do not lend your ears.

A classic example of bad counsel shows up in the Ramayana, where Manthra makes up false narratives to create doubt in the mind of her mistress, Kaikei, regarding the intentions of King Dashrath, Rama and others. She makes Kaikei feel that everyone in the kingdom is secretly scheming against her and her son, Bharata. Kaikei, who previously loved Rama as her own son, develops a deep distrust towards him, and consequently asks Dashrath for a boon to send Rama for a long exile.

Public Opinion

American basketball player, Michael Jordan says, 'Everyday for the rest of your life, you'll have to choose. Do you want to fit in, or do you want embark on the lonely pursuit of greatness?' The unspoken fear, 'What will people say?' influences everyone's life. Public opinion should inform our decisions, not interpolate our decisions. It is good to understand and incorporate popular opinion in one's decision making process but not at the cost of undermining objective evaluation of the situation and tuning into our own needs. If we keep giving in to public opinion all the time, eventually we will stop trusting our own judgement because we shall assume that other people know better.

Activism

The Oxford Dictionary defines activism as 'the policy or action of using vigorous campaigning to bring about political or social change'. Sometimes a group of people wanting a decision to take shape in a particular way may use lobbying and campaigning to influence the decision makers.

In Ramayana, Bharat puts activism to good use to persuade Shri Rama to return to Ayodhya. Shri Rama was stationed at Chitrakoot. Bharat brought an entire entourage of gurus such as Vashishtha, Jabali, their mothers, Kaushalya, Kaykaiyee and Sumitra, ministers such as Sumantra, his entire army and citizens of

Ayodhya to canvas Shri Rama to abandon his vow to stay in the forest. Shri Rama, however, couldn't be swayed by the activism and stated that he was honour bound to fulfill the promise made by his father and could not return to Ayodhya.

Groupthink

Groupthink refers to extreme consensus-seeking tendencies in decision making within a group. People avoid holding any positions or taking any sides lest they may be held responsible for execution of their ideas, judged for their opinions or get implicated in conflict. Playing safe or conflict avoidance becomes the yardstick for decision making in such groups. The result is lack of ownership in the group.

Failure of Consensus

Failure of consensus refers to a situation where there is lack of intent or endeavour towards developing consensus among the stakeholders. This is quite a contrast to groupthink. Consensus is a dynamic way of reaching an agreement between all members of a group. A leader must be collaborative and must take into account everyone's ideas and opinions. Consensus building ensures involvement and support of all team members in the final decision. In the absence of consensus building, team members may feel 'left out' or unwelcome.

Duryodhana's governance in Hastinapura is a classic example of failure of consensus. Dhrtarashtra used to at least ask for counsel from wise ministers like Vidura, though he would never follow it. But his son would always turn a deaf ear to all good advice. He would seek advice only from those whom he knew would endorse his evil plans like Shakuni, Dushasana or Karna.

Situational Complexities

Even if we succeed in keeping all other pitfalls and disablers at bay, there are certain complexities inherent to a situation which can make decision making tough despite our best attempts. Following are some of the situational complexities which one may come across:

1. Information Deficit/Uncertainties
2. Linked Decisions
3. Ethical Paradoxes
4. Inadequate Authority
5. Conflict of Interest

Information Deficit/Uncertainties

Having to take a decision without sufficient information is like cooking a meal without any ingredients. One may put the fire of intelligence to use but if there are no information ingredients, what can one cook? Four levels of uncertainty or information deficit are summed up below:

LEVELS	*Clarity of purpose/ objectives/goals*	*Knowledge of alternatives to achieve the objectives*	*Clarity of outcomes associated with each alternative*
Certainty	High	High	Decent
Risk	High	Decent	Insufficient
Uncertainty	Decent	Insufficient	Vague
Ambiguity	Vague	Vague	Vague

Domino Effect: Linked Decisions

A domino effect or chain reaction is the cumulative effect produced when one event sets off a chain of events. Decisions can lead to such a domino effect and so should be made keeping in mind three dimensions: time, place and people. The effect of decisions tends to get amplified or altered with progression of time, change of place and exposure to more people. Many decisions have a ripple effect and affect one's family, society, nation, etc. Complex situations where one decision is linked to several others call for a broader and long-term vision of the consequences.

Ethical Paradoxes

Tough choices and ethical dilemmas are often very hard to resolve. What makes these decisions hard is that they are often choices of 'right' vs 'right'. Both possibilities have value and merit, yet one must be picked over the other. It is tough when you must choose from some of the following paradoxes:

- Duty or Emotion
- Pragmatic or Idealistic
- Popularity or Purity
- Accommodative or Protective
- Analytical or Intuitive
- Optimistic or Critical
- Authoritative or Collaborative

- Individual or Community
- Mission or Missionary
- Truth or Loyalty
- Short term or Long term
- Justice or Mercy

Inadequate Authority

Sometimes one may be given the onus of making a decision but without sufficient authority to influence the concerned people and execute the decision. It is like being given the steering wheel of a car without access to the accelerator. You can keep manoeuvering the steering wheel but the car won't go anywhere unless you get to press the accelerator.

In the Ramayana, Laxman faces a similar situation. Shri Rama asked him to protect Mother Sita while he was hunting the golden deer. Fearing that Rama was in danger, Sita instructed Laxman to immediately leave and help Rama. However, Laxman was given the responsibility of Sita's protection and so was duty bound to not leave her alone in the hermitage but at the same time he didn't have authority to refuse Mother Sita's instruction.

Conflict of Interest

A conflict of interest is a situation of competing interests or loyalties. There could be a conflict of interest amongst two roles of the same individual or between two different groups over a particular resource. The easiest way to explain the concept of conflict of interest is by using some examples:

- A public official whose personal interests conflict with their professional position.
- A person who has a position of authority in one organisation that conflicts with his or her role in another organisation.
- Interests of two different groups within an organisation in conflict over a particular resource.

DECISION MAKING: ACTIVITY 2

External Challenges in Decision Making—People Pressures & Situational Complexities

Instructions for exercise:

- Select a real-life complex decision situation at an individual, interpersonal or organisational level.
- Below is a list of challenges in decision making which one may encounter if one is not sufficiently watchful. Reflect on your case and ascertain which of the following pitfalls could one fall into while making decisions in such a situation.
- Write a summary of your findings.

People Pressures

People Pressures	*Explanation*	*Possible instance of pitfall in reference to the Case Study provided*
Halo effect/ Relationship bias	• Being influenced by the opinion or interests of a towering personality or a close relationship	
Coercion	• Taking a decision out of force or fear of some powerful person	
Bad counsel	• Being influenced by bad counsel	
Public opinion	• Being influenced by fear of public response	
Activism	• Decision being manipulated by activist lobbying	
Groupthink	• Lack of ownership in a group because of unassigned responsibilities	

People Pressures	*Explanation*	*Possible instance of pitfall in reference to the Case Study provided*
	• Conflict avoidance within the group becoming the objective of decision making	
Failure of consensus	• Not involving the stakeholders • Failing to create consensus amongst stakeholders	

Situational Complexities

Situational Complexities	*Explanation*	*Possible instance of pitfall in reference to the Case Study provided*
Information deficit/ Uncertainties	• Not enough information is available in order to be sure to make a decision	

Situational Complexities	*Explanation*	*Possible instance of pitfall in reference to the Case Study provided*
	• Questions on reliability of available information • Uncertainty about the available alternatives	
Domino effect: Linked decisions	• Complex situations where one decision is linked to several others and can't be viewed in isolation	
Ethical paradoxes	• Choosing between two rights	
Inadequate authority	• One may have been given the onus of decision making without sufficient authority to influence others and execute the decision	
Conflict of interest	• Multiple stakeholders with conflicting interests	

ENABLERS IN DECISION MAKING: HEAD, HEART AND HANDS

We all have experience of situations where we have been through a tug of war between two choices in our life. On one end we are being pulled by the head with convincing logic and reasoning and on the other by the heart with compelling emotions and sentiments. The call of head and heart start vehemently advocating into either of our ears with the tempo building up gradually and eventually the sheer noise of this internal altercation deafens our decision-making abilities, leaving us unable to make any sense of the contradicting voices.

Emotion and reason are integral aspects of the human personality. Since the 17th century, when Descartes proclaimed, 'I think, therefore I am,' science began to consider the rational self as the real self over and above the emotional or sensory self. This belief was in vogue until recently when Antonio Damasio, one of the world's leading neurologists, published Descartes' Error in 1995. Damasio's work and further research by neurobiologists show how emotions and rationality are deeply intertwined and mutually complimenting.

Some people display a predominance of either the rational or emotional element while others have a mix of the two. Let's see the impact of these two elements on someone's personality. Rationality can be understood to function linearly while emotions have a wave-like sinusoidal nature. Logic, being linear, is predictable but its predictability can make it monotonous and dry. However, the predictability and steadiness of the rational element makes the person reliable. On the other hand, the waveform nature of emotions, adds unpredictability and colour to a person's personality, with the drawback of making the person unreliable in situations of high emotional turmoil. An analogy can be helpful to understand these two faculties. Emotions are like the flowing water of a river while rationality is like the banks of the river. The goal of emotionality and rationality is to realise the journey of a person's life to ultimately become a person possessing divine oceanic qualities.

The waters of the river are wave-like, with ripples and flow while the banks are straight and give direction to the water to flow towards its destination, i.e., the ocean. Imagine if there were no banks or weak banks. The water would indiscriminately flood anything that came in its way, would have no direction and wouldn't know how to reach the ocean. On the other hand, if there were only banks with no water, what would the purpose of such banks be? Undoubtedly, we would call such a river dry and useless. Similarly in our life, we need the banks of logic and reason to discriminate and direct us towards our desired destination but at the same time, if the water of emotions is not flowing through, what would be the purpose of such dry logic and reasoning? Thus, a balanced person is one with developed rationality (head) and evolved emotions (heart). Furthermore, along with head and heart we also need determined hands to execute the decisions arrived at. Otherwise, they simply remain wishes. In fact, latest research in neuroscience tell us that we have three brains.[12] The conventional understanding of brain is the 'head' or cephalic brain. However, we also have a heart (cardiac) and a gut (enteric) brain. Each of these three brains have sensory neurons, motor neurons, ganglia and neurotransmitters. In fact, they can all do the brainy functions, i.e., collect information, process it, store it and recall it when needed.

Each of these three brains specialises in a unique function. Our head or cephalic brain is the seat of creativity and is responsible for cognitive perception and logical reasoning. Our heart or cardiac brain defines values, processes emotions and handles relationships. And our gut or enteric brain is a seat of determination and courage and is concerned about self-preservation and self-esteem. You cannot take sound decisions while being disconnected from either your heart or your gut. Great leaders look at what the numbers and analysis have to tell them but also listen to their heart and sense their gut, for arriving at decisions. Thus, we need a three-pronged Head-Heart-Hand approach to decision making.

Let me share with you the H3 (Head Heart Hand) Decision-Making Process. In order to elucidate the process, I shall be sharing some instances of brilliant decisions made by Lord Krishna which led the Pandavas to prevail over the Kauravas in the battle of Kurukshetra.

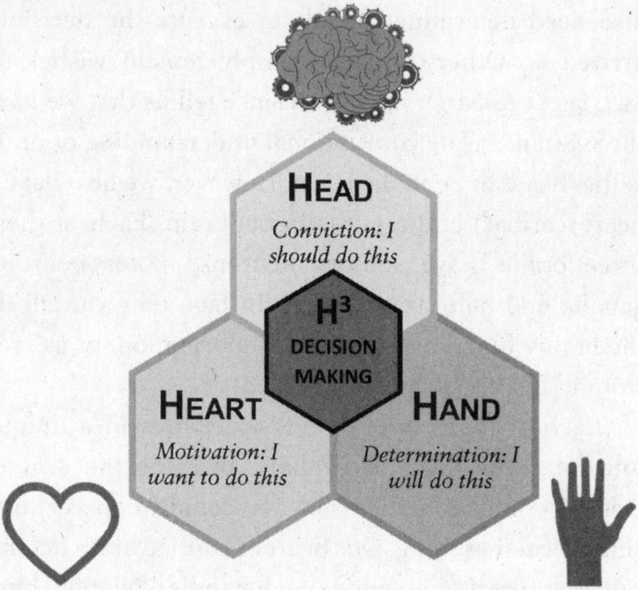

Heads-Up Decision Making

Good decisions are said to be the ones which are well informed and are objectively evaluated, in the backdrop of available information. Following are the components of heads-up decision making:

- **Flexibility:** Keeping aside any fixed ideas/assumptions/prejudices and adapting as per needs.
- **Objectivity:** Objectively evaluating various scenarios and solutions based on the yardstick of principles and values.
- **Creativity:** Conceiving of innovative approaches and alternative solutions.

Krishna displayed flexibility, objectivity and creativity at several instances in the battle.

Flexibility: He had taken a vow to not lift any weapons during the battle of Kurukshetra, but seeing Bhishma's wrathful attack on Arjuna, Krishna lifted a chariot wheel, which is technically not a weapon but can still act as one. Thus, Krishna demonstrated that a leader should be flexible in face of unwarranted situations.

Objectivity: Though Krishna had full faith in Arjuna's ability to defeat Karna, he didn't minimise the threat from Karna. Karna had the powerful Shakti weapon which he had reserved for killing Arjuna. Krishna induced Karna to exhaust his Shakti weapon against Ghatotkacha on the 14th day. Thus, Krishna objectively evaluated all scenarios and proactively eliminated situations which could be harmful for Arjuna.

Creativity: There are umpteen instances where Krishna averted danger by creatively deploying alternative solutions. On being incited by Duryodhana, Bhishma took a vow to kill all the Pandavas and reserved five arrows to kill them. Not trusting Bhishma, Duryodhana asked to keep the arrows in his custody. Understanding that there was no way the Pandavas could survive being shot with these arrows, Krishna decided to seize these arrows from Duryodhana by some means. Krishna woke up Arjuna in the middle of the night and reminded him of the boon Duryodhana owed him. Krishna asked Arjuna to go to Duryodhana and ask for the arrows in lieu of the pending boon. Thus, Krishna creatively averted the lurking threat to the Pandava's lives.

Heart-ful Decision Making

We do need to listen to our hearts and assay the world of our emotions to ensure that the decisions we make won't spring any surprise reactions from our inner world. Our emotions act like an internal GPS—indicating our internal stand or locus-standi with respect to the issue or problem at hand. We need to also stand in the shoes of other stakeholders and visualise their preferences with respect to the available decision alternatives. Following are the components of Heart-ful decision making:

- **Sensitivity:** Being intuitive and feeling the pulse of the people and situation with all nuances.
- **Equanimity:** Keeping one's composure and not being swayed by polarities.
- **Connectivity:** Being friendly and approachable. Taking the team along and building consensus.

Krishna demonstrated heart-ful decision making especially on the 14th day—the day Jayadratha was killed.

Equanimity: Arjuna was greatly incensed by the deceitful killing of Abhimanyu and losing his composure, vowed to kill Jayadratha or enter fire on the 14th day. Krishna reminded Arjuna of the knowledge of the Bhagavad Gita and asked him to remain equipoised. Krishna expertly manoeuvered the chariot through the formation of the Kauravas meant to thwart Arjuna's attempt at reaching Jayadratha. He asked Arjuna to stay equanmious and focused on the goal of reaching Jaydratha and not get distracted by provocative challenges of warriors on the way.

Sensitivity: After racing all day long, Arjuna's horses become very tired and thirsty. Understanding the anguish of the horses, Krishna asks Arjuna to pause the chase for Jayadatha at this critical juncture. Krishna tended to the horses, massaged their tired legs and fed them cool water and grass. With renewed energy and gratitude, the horses sprung back into action and helped Arjuna reach Jayadratha. Thus, Krishna underscored the role of sensitivity in decision making. Time was of utmost essence in the chase of Jayadrtha but by halting the chase to rejuvenate the horses, Krishna was highlighting that though it is important to meet deadlines, people should not drop dead in the chase for deadlines.

Connectivity: Krishna was approachable and trusted by everyone in the Pandava camp. The difference between the Kaurava and Pandava camp was that in face of differences the Kauravas didn't have an accepted leader to help resolve their differences. Pandavas too had their share of misunderstandings and conflicts, but they would unanimously turn to Krishna and put trust in his wisdom and guidance. The Pandava camp was split into two factions on the deceitful killing of Drona. However, Krishna helped iron out the differences and brought everyone on the same page. In another instance, a bitter war of words ensued between Yudhishtira and Arjuna as the elder brother accused Arjuna of being fearful of Karna. Krishna saved the day by giving appropriate advice and diffused the situation.

Hands-On Decision Making

This is where the ignition takes place. The decisions see the light of the day when determined hands pursue and persevere. Following are the components of Hands-on decision making:

- **Bravery:** Being courageous and ready to take risks as required.
- **Agility:** Responding in real time.
- **Tenacity:** Resolving to stick and execute the decision and not keep oscillating.

Bravery: A leader needs to take tough decisions at times and if the context is that of a war, tremendous amounts of courage and risk-taking are required. The decision to put at stake the lives of sons of Pandavas, Abhimanyu, Iravan and Ghatotkacha in the ultimate interest of the Pandavas was definitely a tough decision, fraught with risks. But Krishna knew that such risk taking was essential to ultimately check the Kauravas' generals.

Agility: Krishna demonstrated great agility in decision making too. Three powerful weapons had the potential to change the destiny of the Kurukshetra war, but Krishna changed the destiny of these weapons in the blink of an eye. On the 12th day of the war, Bhagadatta fired the super-weapon, Vaishnava astra, on Arjuna. Before Arjuna could counter this weapon, however, Krishna intervened by standing up at the charioteer's position. Krishna let his chest be a cushion to protect Arjuna. The Vaishnava astra, being a weapon of Vishnu, turned into a garland and fell on Krishna, thus Arjuna's life was saved. The Naag astra shot by Karna had the potential to kill Arjuna. Seeing the deadly weapon approach, Krishna thumped the chariot down with his foot so that it sunk into the ground and the missile whisked past, above Arjuna's head. Finally, the Narayan astra shot by Ashvatthama had no countermeasure and the only defense was to bow down in front of the missile. Krishna immediately made the Pandava army prostrate themselves in front of the weapon and even forced defiant the Bhima to bow down. Thus, Krishna's alertness and agility helped protect the Pandavas from these three super-weapons.

Tenacity: Were it not for the motivation given by Krishna, the Pandavas would have lost steam at various junctures and gone back on their decision to stand up for righteousness. The disrobing of Draupadi, denial of their rightful kingdom and attempts to kill them were reasons enough for the Pandavas to avenge the crimes of Duryodhana and company but considering kinship, they were at times reluctant to engage in an all-out war. Krishna's message of the Bhagavad Gita helped them stick to the path of virtue and the mission of eliminating vice.

Thus, holistic decision making is a 3x3 matrix as depicted in the diagram below:

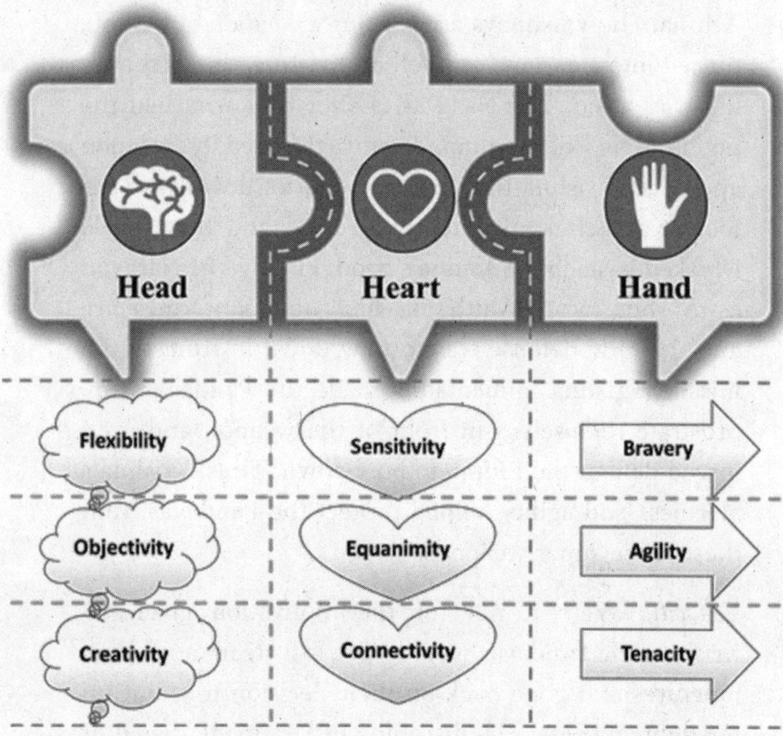

TEN-STEP DECISION-MAKING PROCESS

We have translated the H^3 (Head Heart Hand) Decision-Making Process into ten practical steps:

1. Prepare a broad problem statement
2. Define your identity/ies and role/s with regard to the problem (in case of multiple identities make a priority list)
3. Identify your key objectives and purpose
4. Identify psychological blind spots or social pressures which may distort your decision-making ability
5. Identify the stakeholders and understand the aspirations and apprehensions of the stakeholders
6. Develop a range of good, creative alternatives considering your objectives and the viewpoints of stakeholders
7. Incorporate effect of uncertainty in the potential alternatives to gauge their results or outcomes
8. Distance yourself from the situation emotionally and check whether judgment is being affected by undue psychological blind spots or social pressures
9. In light of all the above considerations, judge the alternatives and make your decision
10. Stick to and execute the decision

DECISION MAKING: ACTIVITY 3

H^3 (Head Heart Hand) Decision-Making Process

Instructions for the exercise:

- Select a real-life complex decision situation at either an individual, interpersonal or organisational level.
- Run your decision situation through the H^3 decision-making process to arrive at a reasonably sound decision. Please fill your responses in the boxes provided in the sheet.
- Make a presentation about the decision situation, objectives, alternatives, the decision arrived at and their experience of following the process.

Step 1:

Broad problem statement:

Step 2:

Your identity/ies and role/s wrt the problem (In case of multiple identities make a priority list)

#	Identity—Role
1	
2	
3	

Step 3:

Your purpose statement:

Key objectives with respect to the problem:

Step 4:

Personal psychological blind spots or social pressures which may distort your decision-making ability:

Step 5:

Major stakeholders and their aspirations and apprehensions:

#	Stakeholder name (Person/ Group)	Aspirations from the decision	Apprehensions about the decision
1			
2			
3			
4			
5			

Step 6:

Wide range of good, creative alternatives considering your objectives and viewpoints of stakeholders:

#	Alternatives	On a scale of 1 to 10 how well it fulfills your objectives	On a scale of 1 to 10 how well it satisfies the stake-holders	On a scale of 1 to 10 determine the feasibility
1				
2				
3				
4				
5				

Step 7:

Factoring influence of uncertainty on the potential alternatives:

#	Alternatives	Associated uncertainities	Modified alternatives in face of uncertainities
1			
2			
3			
4			
5			

Step 8:

Distance yourself from the situation emotionally and check whether your judgment is being affected by undue psychological blind spots or social pressures.

Step 9:

In light of all the above considerations, judge the alternatives and formulate your decision:

Step 10:

Steps needed to execute the decision:

#	Steps	By whom	By when
1			
2			
3			
4			
5			
6			
7			
8			
9			
10			

5. LEADERSHIP 101

Take Your Organisation on a Roll with the Chariot Model of Leadership

Leadership permeates all spheres of human life—one can be the leader of a family, community, society, nation and, of course, one's own self. In the book *Developing the Leader Within You,* author John C. Maxwell writes, 'Sociologists tell us that even the most introverted individual will influence ten thousand other people during his or her lifetime!'[13] Thus, everyone occupies a position of leadership, small or big, and so it is important for each one of us to understand the science of leadership.

Corporations and governments have manpower, machine, material, money and methods but the critical factor which translates these 5 Ms into success is good leadership. Humans, in any walk of life, could be an aimless herd without a leader at helm. In the Ramayana, sage Vashishtha speaks about the importance of a good leader at helm of the state and urges Dashrath to quickly coronate Rama by stating, 'Oh king! Give orders quickly for Rama's coronation ceremony. A kingdom without a king is like cattle without a herdsman, army without a commander and night without the moon.' A leader co-creates a vision with the group, draws inspiration from the group for the vision and invokes their commitment, thus channelising everyone's energy for collective growth.

THE CHARIOT MODEL OF LEADERSHIP

A picture speaks more than a thousand words. It is difficult to picturise an abstract and complex subject such as leadership into one picture but there is one iconic image which can capture all the nuances of leadership succinctly—the picture of Arjuna's chariot being driven by Shri Krishna on the battlefield of Kurukshetra. To emerge victorious in a war despite being the underdogs, despite being outnumbered by the mighty Kaurava army and despite having a history of being manipulated and victimised, could not have been possible without outstanding leadership at helm. In this chapter, we will decipher different aspects of the picture of Shri Krishna guiding Arjuna to victory and in doing so also unravel the mysteries of leadership. I call this the chariot model of leadership.

Here Arjuna represents the heroic manager who is acting under the guidance of the virtuous leader, Shri Krishna. Let me clarify the difference between leadership and management before we move ahead. Leadership means 'the ability of an individual to inspire, influence, and enable others to contribute toward a common cause by personal volition'. On the other hand, management involves 'governing and directing a group of people or entities for the purpose of accomplishing a goal'. Both leadership and management are indispensable functions and it is important to understand that one is not a replacement for the other. However, without leadership, management shall remain ineffective and cumbersome. The following table enlists some of the differences between leadership and management:

Characteristics	*Leadership*	*Management*
Driving force	Cause/Purpose	Success/Results
Appeals to	Heart	Head
Horizon	Long term	Short term
Direction	Sets vision	Sets targets
Modelling	Sets example	Sets policies
Organisation culture	Shapes culture	Administers/enacts culture
Decision-making	Facilitative	Involved
Orientation	People-oriented	Process-oriented
Styles	Transformational, consultative and participative	Dictatorial, authoritative, transactional, autocratic, consultative and democratic
Relationship/Bond	Informally through inspiration and example (create circle of influence/ inspiration)	Formally through authority and position (create circle of power/ authority)
Organisation	Leaders have followers	Managers have subordinates

The combination of a competent manager like Arjuna and a conscious leader like Shri Krishna is the recipe for organisational success. Let us see what brilliance a conscious leader like Shri Krishna can bring to the table.

CLEAR VISION AND PURPOSE

At sunrise on the first day of the battle of Kurukshetra, Arjuna seemed to be quite in command of himself and the situation. Like a seasoned warrior, he asked Krishna to draw the chariot in between the armies so that he could survey the situation and formulate the best strategy for impending war. The chariot was drawn right in the midst of the battlefield and Arjuna closely surveyed the armies which included his dear relatives and friends on both sides. At this juncture, the so-far equipoised Arjuna became poignant and experienced unexpected PTSD with his limbs quivering, mouth drying up, hair standing on end, skin burning and bow slipping from his hand. Why did this happen? What went wrong? In the fast-paced world today, we often rush into setting targets, formulating strategies and mobilising resources, without at first clarifying the purpose and vision—the consequence being that you may find yourself and your team ending up in a state of confusion and vacillation, as had happened with Arjuna.

To his credit, Arjuna had chosen to have the unarmed visionary, Shri Krishna, on his side over the firepower of the Narayani Sena, an army of a million battle-hardened warriors. This choice very subtly gives the mathematical implication of the importance of vision over other factors—a million is to one, which made its preeminence count at different junctures of the 18-day battle but especially in the beginning as Shri

Krishna spoke the message of Bhagavad Gita to dissipate the fog of Arjuna's indecision. The message of the Gita clarified the vision and purpose for Arjuna and gave him the perspective and motivation to do his duty—the battle was now no longer a family feud between cousin brothers or a means to establish supremacy but a struggle to establish good over evil, to eliminate exploitation and oppression and to hoist the flag of righteousness and freedom. As it is said, for someone who has won over the battles within, victory in battles without is but a consequence. This is the power of a clear vision.

French aviator and author of the early 20th century, Antoine De Saint-Exupery, once said, 'If you want to build a ship, then don't drum up men to gather wood, give orders, and divide the work. Rather, teach them to yearn for the far and endless sea.' Great leaders have a worthy cause at the heart of their endeavours. They try to bring the cause into the limelight rather than being in the limelight themselves. History is replete with examples of leaders who have worked for diverse causes—social, political, economic, philanthropic, spiritual, etc.:

- Fraternity and human rights: Mahatma Gandhi, Martin Luther King
- Poverty/disease alleviation: Oprah Winfrey, Baba Amte
- Spiritual upliftment: Saint Francis of Assisi, Swami Prabhupada

- Innovation/economic growth: Henry Ford, Elon Musk
- Sports excellence: Michael Jordan, M.S. Dhoni

It is such a cause which forms the basis for the leader to bring everyone together and pool in their talents and resources to realise that cause.

Communicating the Vision

Great leaders have the ability to visualise a shared, meaningful purpose which resonates with the aspirations of their people and helps knit them together in one unit. Further, they communicate the purpose in an inspiring way with the effect that people start owning the purpose, rather than borrowing it or going along with it. What are some of the features of communication about the cause or vision which create the required acceptance and inspiration?

1. **Visualisation:** Evoke a clear and positive mental image of the future
2. **Motivation:** Appeal to the head and heart. Gives a sense of meaning and accomplishment
3. **Identification:** Reflect the values of the organisation, aspirations of its people and makes the organisation stand out from the crowd
4. **Direction:** Lay out a path leading from current state to future state and act as a compass for decision making

5. **Call for action:** Move people to action in the here and now

Bob Nelson, an expert on motivation theory says, 'You get the best effort from others not by lighting a fire beneath them, but by building a fire within.' However one can't light a flame in another person's heart if it is not there in one's own heart. Leaders personally identify with the cause and go all out for it. With such fire of commitment in their own hearts, they naturally draw commitment from others. When people develop a sense of belonging to the cause, following behaviours manifest in the organisation:

- People start taking ownership and initiative
- Improvisation and innovation pick up
- Need for formal motivational mechanisms like hierarchy, rules, legislation, targets, deadlines, etc. reduces as people give their best anyway even without a system of appraisal in place
- Bureaucracy and politics get sidelined
- Monotonous daily activities attain meaning and significance
- Every one's contribution gets recognised and respected
- Synergy increases as people become willing to extend themselves and sacrifice their egos for the greater good

Getting People to Rise Up to See the Vision

The vision of the leader may be very exalted, but if they don't take the effort to uplift the people to a level from where they can spot that vision, it will remain obscure and irrelevant for them. Even though the leader may personally have high ideals and a sacred purpose which drives them, they will not be able to mobilise people for that sacred purpose unless the consciousness and motivations of the subordinates also get tuned to those of the leader. Thus, it is of paramount importance for leaders to work on raising the level of consciousness and motivation of the people they lead. What people are motivated by, depends on what they identify themselves with, i.e., the anchor of their consciousness Therefore, Shri Krishna took the effort to have a detailed philosophical discussion at an unlikely place, i.e., the battlefield. He began his message to Arjuna by uplifting the anchor of his consciousness from bodily consciousness to spiritual consciousness (Bhagavad Gita 2.12-28).

Depending on where one's anchor of consciousness lies, one's motivation or driving forces will be decided. Stable, sustainable and successful leadership entails gradually raising the consciousness and the corresponding motivations of the followers from grossly selfish realms to higher, evolved realms of human existence. The following table lists different consciousness anchors and the concomitant motivational factors:

#	*Consciousness Levels*	*Motivational Factors*
1	**Fear Consciousness**	Policy of hire and fire, performance appraisals
2	**Reward Consciousness**	Bonuses, performance-based remittance, fringe benefits, career growth
3	**Emotional Fulfilment Consciousness**	Work-life balance, sabbaticals, team outings, acknowledgment of contributions and sharing credit, various forms of employee care
4	**Self-worth Consciousness**	Stimulating challenges at work and concomitant appreciation/ recognition/ awards
5	**Duty Consciousness**	Cultivating sense of belonging and ownership amongst followers for the organisation and their role within the organisation, nominate best practice owners
6	**Knowledge Consciousness**	Learning opportunities, freedom and facility for experimentation and innovation, training programs
7	**Service Consciousness**	Cultivating spirit of selfless sacrifice and service for a higher purpose/cause

If the primary motivational tool which the organisation/society is used to is fear, then the organisation/society as a whole will also be crippled by fear consciousness, which in the long run is neither stable nor successful, though it may see quick returns initially. Motivational tools completely based in lower levels of consciousness may eventually backfire in the form of employee burnouts, dissatisfaction, attrition, etc.

On the other hand, if the primary motivation of the organisation/society is that of serving together towards a higher cause then it will be fueled by an unparalleled commitment and passion for fulfilling the higher cause. Such motivation being rooted in a selfless cosmic consciousness will yield zeal and results amongst the followers, unmatched by motivations rooted in any of the limited forms of consciousness. Although developing such consciousness at the organisational level requires great investment from the leadership and also takes time to blossom, when it sprouts, it pays off great dividends. In fact, organisations/societies grounded in a consciousness of service are truly stable and, in the long term, sustainable, i.e. built to last.

LEADERSHIP 101: ACTIVITY 1

Great leaders have a worthy cause at the heart of their endeavours. Articulate your vision or purpose statement which will motivate and spur you and your team into action:

Subject the above vision statement to the test of following parameters and rate on a scale of 1 to 5:

#	Parameter	Explanation	Rating (1 to 5)
1	Visualisation	Does it evoke a clear and positive mental image of the future?	
2	Motivation	Does it appeal to the head and heart and give a sense of meaning and accomplishment?	

#	Parameter	Explanation	Rating (1 to 5)
3	Identification	Does it reflect the values of the organisation, aspirations of its people and makes the organisation stand out from the crowd?	
4	Direction	Does it lay out a path leading from current state to future state and acts as a compass to take decisions?	
5	Call for action	Does it move people to action in the here and now?	

The above ratings will give you a clue on which parameters does your articulated vision fall short. Refine the vision statement, so as to take care of the deficiencies:

INSPIRING VALUES AND VIRTUES

What constitutes the fabric of the relationship between a leader and their followers? What material is it made up of? Is it organisational hierarchy or some other sort of compulsion which binds them together? If any form of compulsion were in play, then you would really not need a leader—a supervisor or manager would suffice. A leader is someone who doesn't necessarily need formal position, authority or compensation to influence their people. In our chariot model of leadership, the horses of Arjuna's chariot represent the people in the organisation and the reins of these horses represents the influence which drives them. Interestingly the reigns of the horses are in the hands of Shri Krishna, the position-less leader and not Arjuna, the officially appointed manager. Thus, people are driven to extend themselves beyond their comfort zones, being inspired by a caring, virtuous leader and not necessarily by dangling carrots and wrangling sticks. To this extent, when the managers emulate the sacred values and principles, they are able to exert positive influence on their subordinates and followers.

Leadership is associated with the words like magnetism, gravitation and so on, which means it is a force which acts invisibly and creates visible transformations. Unlike contact forces which need physical contact for exertion, magnetism and gravitation are non-contact forces and don't need physical contact for the same. This holds true for leadership as well. A leader's influence can act with or without any formal title or any extrinsic compulsion like fear or reward.

Shri Krishna's personality gives a glimpse into the characteristics of an effective leader. Krishna never accepted any formal leadership role but as it turns out, he always naturally emerges as the most popular leader in all situations. It is quite interesting to note that Krishna declined to lift arms in the iconic battle of Kurukshetra but is nonetheless celebrated as the decisive hero of the battle. Earlier on in his life, Krishna dethroned the tyrant Kamsa and it was expected that he would take over the kingdom of Mathura but instead, he reinstated Ugrasena, Kamsa's father, as the king of the Vrshni clan. However, even without any formal position, he always played a pivotal role in steering the Vrshnis out of all situations of crisis, conflict and conspiracy such as the attacks of Jarasandha, Kalayavana, Shalva, Shyamantaka conspiracy, etc. A nuanced study of Krishna's character reveals that leadership is not dependent on exercising instruments such as position, rewards or punishment.

Leadership is about creating an environment charged with inspiration. The invisible bond between the leader and the followers is that of inspiration and the leader influences them to engage in certain behaviours by strength of that inspiration. What evokes this inspiration in people towards a leader has been a subject of study for thinkers and researchers throughout the world. To understand this we would need to delve into the thoughts, words and actions of great leaders.

Thoughts—Concern

Feeling the 'vibes' of a room or person is a common human experience. Studies have shown that humans tend to intuitively sense emotional energy emitted by other people. If they perceive vibes of goodwill and trust, they will orient themselves favourably to strike up a relationship. On the other hand, vibes of selfishness, exploitation or disrespect result in people withdrawing themselves. A true leader has genuine concern and respect for the people around them which is reflected in their words and actions. Robert Greenleaf, founder of the servant leadership movement, states that the greatest value to an organisation comes from a servant leader who 'shares power, puts the needs of others first and helps people develop and perform as highly as possible'. Conventionally, a leader is considered to be someone who instructs and commands the followers to serve in various capacities but a servant leader is someone who genuinely considers themselves to be the servant of every servant in the organisation. They embody first what they expect of others. Even if they instruct or offer some feedback, it is done in a mood of service.

Shri Krishna is such a servant leader whose genuine concern, service and attitude endeared him to everyone's hearts—even those of his horses. On the 14th day of the battle, Arjuna was chasing after Jayadratha to avenge the deceitful killing of Abhimanyu. After racing all day long, Arjuna's horses became very tired and thirsty.

Understanding their anguish, Krishna asked Arjuna to pause the chase for Jayadratha at this critical juncture and make a protective shield around the horses with his arrows. He then tended to the horses, massaged their tired legs and gave them water and grass. With renewed energy and gratitude, the horses sprung back into action and helped Arjuna nail Jayadratha down. Such was the synergy of the horses with Shri Krishna that they would understand and deftly follow his indications. Later on in the battle, when Karna shot the lethal Naag astra at Arjuna, this synergy between Krishna and his horses came to Arjuna's rescue. Seeing the deadly Naag astra approach, Krishna thumped his foot down. Understanding their master's indication, the horses immediately crouched down, thus lowering the chariot as the missile whisked above Arjuna's head. When you genuinely care for your people, they naturally care for you too.

Words—Communication

Communication is a core leadership function. Messages coming from the leadership form the blueprint which shapes the organisation, its goals, its ethos and its structure. Leadership communications should not be distrustful or intimidating. The speech, tone and body language should be inclusive, respectful and cordial. People should feel that the leader is one amongst them and their voices too are represented by them rather than sounding like a dictator who just cracks down orders for the rest to meekly follow. When people sense a distrustful or disrespectful tenor or tone in communications coming from leadership, they will choose either of the two responses:

1. Succumb to inferiority complex, stop believing in themselves and stay stunted. They will at best be yes-men but can't be expected to take responsibilities and initiative
2. Rebel and display uncooperative behaviours. Rebellious behaviours could be staying non-committal and neutral; circumventing decisions of the leadership smartly; creating an adjusted space for one's independent operation; moving out, or worse, staying within the organisation and creating unpleasantness.

Although it is important to learn from mistakes of the past, leadership communications don't hinge around them. Speech of leaders are not meant to create guilt but inspiration. Leaders may use past mistakes as triggers but their focus should be to create an impact on the future so that it is progressive. Please refer to the 9Cs of communication in the chapter on communication skills:

1. Correct: Fact-checked and from authentic sources
2. Consistent: Repeated emphasis
3. Complementary (two-way): Ears first, speech later

4. Cordial: Warm and friendly
5. Concise: Short and sweet
6. Clear: Unambiguous and coherent
7. Contextual: With reference to time, place, person and circumstance
8. Constructive: Coming from a benevolent space of helping others
9. Compelling/ Cause-driven: Accompanied by call for action for a shared purpose

Actions—Conduct

Someone may fake goodwill and may also be able to communicate impressively but won't be able to sustain the inspiration without aligned personal conduct. People hear what you say but also wait to observe what you do and form their opinions and make decisions based on that. Connecting to a leader whose personal conduct doesn't align with their cause is almost impossible. Nobel peace prize winner, Albert Schweitzer, says, 'Example is not the main thing in influencing others. It is the only thing.'

An ancient Indian wisdom text, *Vayu Purana*, gives the definition of a leader or an acharya as one who sets example by personal conduct:

acinoti yah shastrarthan
svacaraih sthapayaty api |
svayam acarate yasmat
tasmad acarya ucyate ||

Such a person is called an acarya or a leader who knows the principles of ideal conduct, behaves in that way himself and inspires his followers to follow the same.

In other words, a leader is someone who knows the way, goes the way and thus, shows the way. One's actions should be in congruence with one's thoughts and words, else one's words will lose value. Another wisdom text, *Padma Purana*, underscores the importance of the quality of integrity in a leader:

manasy ekam vacasy ekam karmany eka mahatmanam |
manasy anyad vacasy anyat
karmany anyad duratmanam ||

Great people are those whose thoughts, words and actions are aligned whereas cripple-minded people are those who think or believe something, say something else and do something else.

Thus, the empathetic concern, engaging communication and ethical conduct of a leader endears them to the followers and inspires them to channelise their emotions, energies and efforts to work towards the shared purpose set by the leader.

Jim Collins, author of the best-selling management book *Good to Great* emphasises that the key ingredient that allows any organisation to become great is having a Level 5 leader: 'an executive in whom genuine personal humility blends with intense determination'. Thus, a Level 5 leader is a very competent executive with a spotless character. Backed up by breakthrough statistical research running over five years for over 100 companies, this research by Jim Collins and his team proves that humility is a defining characteristic of outstanding leaders. Collins states that Level 5 leader sit on top of a hierarchy of capabilities. A full-fledged Level 5 requires the capabilities of all the other levels, plus the special characteristics of Level 5. Let us have a look at the characteristics of a leader at each of these levels:

1. **Level 5 Executive:** Builds enduring greatness through a paradoxical combination of personal humility and professional will.
2. **Level 4 Effective Leader:** Catalyses commitment to and vigorous pursuit of a clear and compelling vision; stimulates the group to high performance standards.
3. **Level 3 Competent Manager:** Organises people and resources toward the effective and efficient pursuit of predetermined objectives.
4. **Level 2 Contributing Team Member:** Contributes to the achievement of group objectives; works effectively with others in a group setting.
5. **Level 1 Highly Capable Individual:** Makes productive contributions through talent, knowledge, skills and good work habits.

A Level 5 leader serves as the ideal example for the team to magnetise itself around and achieve great things together. The personal humility of Level 5 leaders represents a pure heart while professionals represent a perseverant head.

There are two types of values: **head values** and **heart values.** Head values are geared towards performance and results while heart values are geared towards purpose and relationships. Head values ensure that we produce fabulous results while heart values ensure that those results are sustainable and accommodative. Both of these complement each other. Here is a complementary list of head and heart values:

Head Values	Heart Values
Efficiency	Effectiveness
Projects	People
Excellence	Empathy
Expedience/ Promptness	Etiquette
Discipline	Benevolence/ Modeling
Responsibility	Trust
Confidentiality	Transparency
Competence	Character
Institutional Growth	Individual Growth
Success	Succession

A list of inspiring values which define your organisation or project can serve as a compass which can help align thought process, create consensus and arrive at major decisions with clarity.

LEADERSHIP 101: ACTIVITY 2

Creating an Inspired Workplace

Leadership is about creating an environment surcharged with inspiration. The invisible bond between the leader and the followers is that of inspiration and the leader influences them to engage in certain behaviors by strength of that inspiration. In each of the below section on mind, words and actions; rate yourself on a scale of 1 to 5 on how well you create that inspiration by answering the following questions:

Mind—Concern

As a leader do you carry genuine care and concern for the people you lead? Do you keep their interests first before your own? What practical steps can you take on a regular basis to practically demonstrate your concern for them?

Rating (1 to 5):
Steps for Improvement:

Words—Communication

Rate your communication based on the various parameters as mentioned below and write down steps to raise your rating:

#	*Parameters for good communication*	*Rating (1 to 5)*	*Steps to improve*
1	Correct: Fact-checked and from authentic sources		
2	Consistent: Repeated emphasis		
3	Complementary (two-way): Ears first, speech later		
4	Cordial: Warm and friendly		
5	Concise: Short and sweet		
6	Clear: Unambiguous and coherent		
7	Contextual: With reference to time, place, person and circumstance		
8	Constructive: Coming from a benevolent space of helping others		
9	Compelling/Cause-driven: Accompanied by a call for action for a shared purpose		

Actions—Conduct

Are your actions in alignment with your words? Are you recognised as a person of integrity and honesty? What could you do to increase your trustworthiness?

Rating (1 to 5):
Steps for Improvement:

LEADERSHIP 101: ACTIVITY 3
Guiding Values and Virtues

Please make a list of values which can serve as a compass for your organisation or project. The values should reflect the purpose, products and people of your organization and vice versa. Please make sure that your list of values factors in both head and heart values.:

1
2
3
4
5

ROBUST PROCESSES AND SYSTEMS

Leadership is not just about being good to people and speaking of great ideals, but also about applying oneself with diligence and intelligence to set things in motion by building up systems from the grassroot levels. Great leaders not only connect to their people and lay out a grand vision, they also create self-sustaining and self-improvising processes and systems which translate dreams into reality and help make success a habit for the organisation. Chanakya succinctly identifies five components of creating a successful establishment in *Arthashastra* 1.15.42:

- Deliberation on the means of starting an undertaking: *Creating the Blueprint*
- The excellence of men and material: *Resource Allocation*
- Suitable apportionment of place and time: *Strategic Positioning*
- Provision against failure: *Contingency Planning*
- Accomplishment of work: *Execution*

Thus, the job of a leader doesn't stop at creating a vision and blueprint—they must work through with the details to ensure that the dreams are translated into reality. Shri Krishna helped the Pandavas with all the above areas and thus ultimately ensured their victory:

- **Creating the Blueprint:** Shri Krishna was the mastermind behind all the strategies laid down by the Pandavas.

- **Resource Allocation:** Fielding Ghatotkacha against Karna so that the Shakti weapon reserved for killing Arjuna is exhausted.
- **Strategic Positioning:** Sending Arjuna in the night to Duryodhana to fetch the five arrows reserved by Bhishma for killing the Pandavas. Sending Yudhishtira to Bhishma to find out how to slay him in battle.
- **Contingency Planning:** Covering the sun with his *chakra* to dupe Jayadratha to come out in public view and thus become the target of Arjuna's arrow.
- **Execution:** Staging the fall of Bhishma, Drona and Karna.

Donald Tosti, an expert on organisational strategy and systems, says that an organisation is comprised of three main environments:[14]

1. The physical environment: operational systems
2. The social environment: people systems
3. The organisational environment: management systems

As an example, let us consider a restaurant chain. The standardisation of recipes, process flows, stewarding practices, billing, IT desk, branding features, etc., would constitute the physical environment or the operations. Recruitment and training of chefs, work culture, customer care ethos, etc., would constitute the social environment or people systems. Organisational hierarchy, franchise network, communication systems, etc. would fall under the organisational environment or management systems of the restaurant chain. If an organisation is compared to the human body, the physical environment which carries out the operational functions would correspond to the skeletal and muscular systems, social environment which is the heart of any organisation would be akin to the cardiovascular system and organisational environment which is the intelligence activating all the processes and systems would correspond to the nervous system.

Leaders work towards building robust systems for these three environments.

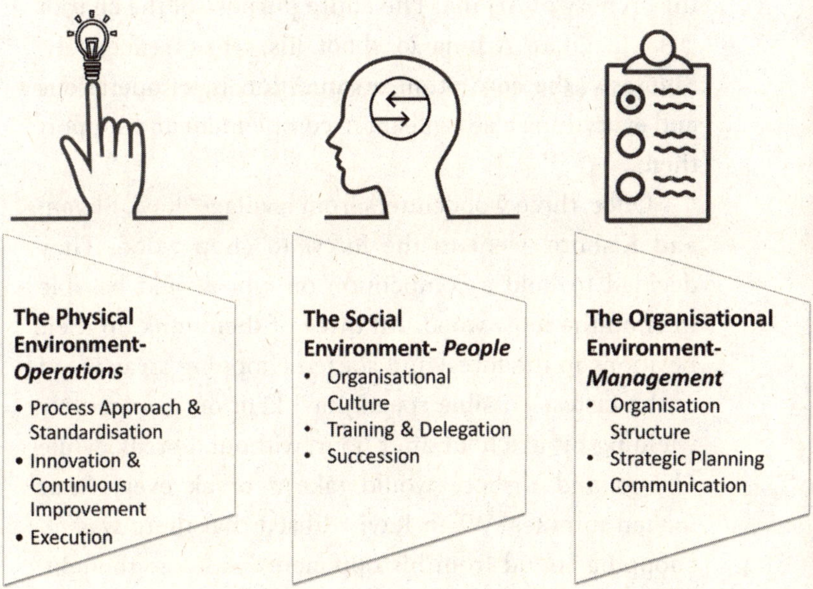

A leader is like an architect or engineer who creates the blueprint for the success of the organisation by building these systems.

The Physical Environment—Operational Systems

The physical environment facilitates the execution of core operations of the organisation. It deals with the workflows, equipment, plant, raw materials, goods, etc. If the physical environment is efficiently designed, it will ensure lower costs, high speed of production, and superior quality of products and thus offer a competitive advantage to your organisation. In our chariot model of leadership, the operational systems are characterised by the archery of Arjuna. The entire purpose of the chariot is to facilitate Arjuna to shoot his arrows effectively. Similarly, the core of an organisation is its operations and everything else is meant to complement and support them.

Once, three woodcutters from a village, Ravi, Shyam and Kishore, went to the forest to chop wood. They decided to hold a competition on who would be able to chop the most wood. All three of them took up their positions in the forest and started chopping away wood at the fastest possible speed. Ravi kept on passionately wielding his axe hour after hour, without a break, while Shyam and Kishore would take a break every hour for ten minutes. When Ravi realised that there was no chopping sound from his opponents' side, he thought: 'Ah ha! They must be tired already!' And he continued to cut down his trees at double the pace. Kishore seemed to take shorter breaks even in between that one hour as there was no chopping sound from his axe for a couple minutes intermittently. When the competition ended, Ravi was absolutely confident that he would be triumphant. But to Ravi's astonishment, Kishore had actually cut down the largest amount of wood, followed by Shyam while he came third, even after spending maximum energy. How did this happen?

'How could both of you have chopped down more trees than me? I heard you stop every hour for ten minutes!' exclaimed Ravi.

Shyam replied, 'Well, it's really simple. Every time I stopped work, while you were still chopping down trees, I was sharpening my axe.' Then Shyam asked Kishore about the secret of his success.

Kishore replied that, 'Like you, I would also stop to sharpen the axe for ten minutes, every hour but I would also stop intermittently to insert and position some wedges into the half-cut wood in order to increase the efficiency of my work.' Thus, though it seemed that Kishore was most spaced out, his work output was maximum because he devoted time and energy to create an efficient workspace or physical environment. The practice of three disciplines contribute to creating an efficient physical environment:

- process approach and standardisation
- innovation and continuous improvement
- execution

Process Approach and Standardisation

The word 'process' is defined as 'a set of interrelated or interacting activities that transforms inputs into outputs'. Process approach is one of the eight quality management principles of ISO 9000:2005. It entails breaking down the organisation's operations into key processes. This breakdown gives a bird's eye view of the organisation's operations as an integrated and complete system constituted of several processes. Once the key processes of the organisation are identified, standards and best practices for each of them are defined and documented. Standardisation of processes helps in making the operations efficient, effective, scalable and replicable. It is the responsibility of the leaders to ensure that the organisation's key processes are captured and documented. Following are some of the losses to the organisation if these are not done:

- Lack of consistency in results
- Inability to adjust to changes in internal and external environment
- Lot of time invested in decision making every time because of lack of standardisation
- Difficulty in scaling up or replicating the operations
- Loss of knowhow and expertise of people when they move out of their position thus losing out on valuable organisational experience
- Painful and resource-intensive reinvention of the wheel

- Inadequate or inefficient cross-functional collaboration
- Frequent conflicts over non-essential issues

Innovation and Continuous Improvement

Innovation is about developing new products, services or processes which have the potential to bring about a drastic jump in efficiency or effectiveness. On the other hand, continuous improvement is the philosophy and practice of undertaking ongoing efforts to improve existing products, services, or processes. Continuous improvement is also one of the eight quality management principles of ISO 9000:2005. Both innovation and continuous improvement spring from the ethos of striving to get better and are essential for the organisation to stay competitive in the fast-evolving world today. Arjuna was always on the lookout to get better at his archery skills and invested a lot of time in learning the skill and acquiring new celestial weapons from the devatas. It is thus the responsibility of leaders to ensure that the ethos of innovation and continuous improvement is permeated in the organisational culture. This can be done in various ways like best practice sharing or by rewarding innovation/improvement.

Execution

Good execution can take a simple idea and turn it into profitable successful business. Bad execution, however, can ruin a brilliant idea and turn it into a pile of debts and a bunch of burnt-out people. Ram Charan, co-author of *Execution: The Discipline of Getting Things Done,* states, 'Seventy percent of strategic failures are due to poor execution. It is rarely for lack of smarts or vision.' Business tycoon Warren Buffet, says, 'You don't have to be smarter than the rest, you have to be more disciplined than the rest.' It takes incredible discipline on part of the organisation to execute its strategic plans. Great leaders lay great emphasis on seamless execution of strategic plans. Chanakya talks about a four-level approach to execution: 'The leader should bring about the commencement of what is not done, the carrying out of what is commenced, the improvement of what is being carried out and the excellence of the execution of orders, in the case of works' (*Arthashastra* 1.15.51). The detailed process of strategic planning and execution has been discussed elaborately in a separate chapter.

The Social Environment—People Systems

Chanakya says, 'Rulership can be successfully carried out only with the help of associates. One wheel alone does not turn. Therefore, he should appoint ministers and listen to their opinion' (*Arthashastra* 1.7.9). Just as a vehicle cannot run on one wheel, similarly a leader cannot pull through the organisation alone. Leadership is not a unilateral entreaty—it is a collaborative endeavour where the leader inspires the team to join in for collaborative effort. Thus, creating a conducive social environment is an essential function of leadership.

A leader should be a great team worker and team builder. They should know how to work in teams, how to make teams work together and how to create a conducive environment for the teams to do so. In our leadership chariot analogy, the people systems are represented by the horses and the troops accompanying Arjuna. The presence of Shri Krishna created an environment of synergy and understanding in the Pandava camp where everyone respected the contribution of others while performing their parts perfectly. While the math was in favour of the Kauravas (eleven Aksauhini divisions over seven divisions of the Pandavas), the chemistry was definitely in favour of the Pandavas. The Kaurava camp was studded with mighty warriors but with explosive chemistry between them—Bhishma and Karna had mutual contempt for each other and would not fight if the other one was in the army, Shakuni's hidden intention was destruction of the entire Kaurava clan, Bhishma and Drona didn't approve of the characterless Jayadratha, Shalya and Karna also had mutual contempt for each other. On the other hand, the Pandavas worked together as a team and even though there were misunderstandings among them, they were ameliorated by the counsel of Shri Krishna who was loved and respected by one and all. There was anger and bitterness in the heart of Arjuna and Satyaki over the way Dhrsthadyumna killed Drona.

Similarly, Yuddhishtira and Arjuna squabbled when the latter came to Yuddhishtira without killing Karna. While Duryodhana's selfishness acted as a catalyst for explosive reactions in the Kaurava camps, it was Shri Krishna's loving counsel which cooled the heated situations down and helped sense and synergy to prevail in the Pandava camp. Therefore, it is essential for that a leader pays attention to creating a harmonious social environment.

How can a leader create a conducive social environment where the team can thrive and succeed? Through the practice of the following three disciplines:

1. Organisational culture
2. People development
3. Succession planning

Organisational Culture

Research by Deloitte reveals several interesting findings about how workplace culture affects the organisation's success.[15] The research states that 94% of executives and 88% of employees believe that a distinct corporate culture is important to a business' success. The research shows that there is a significant correlation between employees who say they are 'happy at work' and feel 'valued by [their] company' and those who say their organisation has a clearly articulated and lived culture. However, there seems to be a disconnect between employees' perception of their workplace culture and that of the executives. When considering what factors impact workplace culture, executives rank tangible elements such as financial performance (65%) and competitive compensation (62%) among the highest, whereas those factors were among the lowest for employees. In contrast, employees rank intangible elements such as regular and candid communication (50%), employee recognition (49%) and access to management/leadership (47%) highest.

Here we have listed down essential features of a good organisational environment:

1. Transparency over Bureaucracy: Culture of Open Communication
2. Trust over Insecurity: Culture of Empowerment
3. Empathy over Apathy: Culture of Personalism
4. Excellence over Mediocrity: Culture of Diligence
5. Meritocracy over Nepotism: Culture of Rewarding Excellence
6. Appreciation over Criticism: Culture of Encouragement (Catching people doing right more often than wrong)
7. Inclusiveness over Apartheidism or Monopoly: Culture of Respect
8. Interdependence over Individualism or Groupthink: Culture of Collaboration

If we compare the Pandava and Kaurava armies, we can clearly see that the Pandava camp enjoyed an open and empowering culture as described above as opposed to the culture of the Kaurava camp which was bureaucratic and competitive.

Embedding the Desired Culture

Building organisational culture is a great science. There are three laws which govern organisational culture in a scientifically precise way. Let's take a look at the three Laws of Culture:

- Culture invisibly influences the visible and the invisible.
- Either you manage culture or culture manages you.
- Whatever leaders do and don't do creates culture.

Culture Invisibly Influences the Visible and the Invisible

Organisational culture is like an iceberg which has a small visible component but a major portion is invisible, hidden below the waters. The visible component is comprised of behaviuors, customs, practices, protocols etc. Behind those visible behaviours are values, some spoken and some unspoken, which shape them. However, the unseen, massive chunk of the culture iceberg is the assumptions, outlook, mindset, etc., which are submerged way under the waters. These assumptions are like the invisible roots which give rise to the trunk of values and fruits of behaviours.

Either You Manage Culture or Culture Manages You

It takes conscious, determined effort to create and maintain the desired culture. Assumptions and behaviours constitute self-feeding cycles. Assumptions shape behaviour; behaviour shapes assumptions. The way we see the world (assumptions) determines what we do (behaviour), what we do determines what we get (results), what we get determines what we see (assumptions). One could either lurk in vicious cycles of unwanted assumptions shaping detrimental behaviours or consciously trigger virtuous cycles where proper behaviours shape desirable assumptions. Thus, you can consciously manage culture or let culture manage you.

Whatever Leaders Do and Whatever Leaders Don't Do Creates Culture

It is neither feasible nor possible to compel everyone in the organisation to start practicing the desired behaviours by power of legislation or rewards. The most effective way to turn around organisational culture is through the examples set by leaders. The example set by the leaders is closely observed and followed by everyone else. Interestingly, whatever leaders do and whatever they don't do creates culture. Culture is thus not taught but it is caught by seeing the right example.

Edgar Schein, in his book *Organizational Culture and Leadership*[16] speaks of primary and secondary mechanisms which help in embedding culture in an organisation:

1. **Primary Embedding Mechanisms**
   a. Observed criteria by which leaders allocate rewards and status.
   b. That which leaders pay attention to, measure and evaluate on a regular basis.
   c. How leaders react to critical incidents and organisational crises.
   d. Observed criteria by which leaders allocate resources, especially when scarce.
   e. Observed criteria by which leaders recruit, select, promote, retire and exclude members.
   f. Deliberate role modelling, teaching and coaching.

2. **Secondary Articulation and Reinforcement Mechanisms**
   a. Design of physical space, facades and buildings.
   b. Stories, legends and myths about people and events.
   c. Formal statements of organisational philosophy, values and creed.
   d. Organisation design and structure.
   e. Organisational systems and procedures.
   f. Organisational rites and rituals.

If we closely observe, all the primary culture embedding mechanisms are based on the behaviours and examples set by the leaders.

People Development

People development has three components: 1) identification of talent, 2) training in skills and values and 3) delegation of responsibilities. When these functions are executed properly, projects automatically become successful. While asking Bharat about the welfare of Ayodhya, Shri Rama gives deep insights people development (*Ramayana* 2.100):

- **Diligence in recruitment:**
  - **Character First:** *I hope you are appointing those ministers who are incorruptible and who are full of integrity in matters of great importance.*
  - **Quality over Quantity (Competence):** *Even if a king employs thousands or tens of thousands of fools, they will not be helpful to him. Even one wise, valiant and efficient minister alone can cause to secure a great prosperity to the king.*
  - **Positive Attitude and Team work:** *I hope an army-chief who is cheerful, wise, courageous, valiant, well-behaved, born in a good family, who is beloved by his subordinates and efficient, is selected by you.*
- **Appropriate job allocation:** *I hope that superior servants are assigned superior work only, mediocre servants for mediocre work and inferior servants for inferior work.*
- **Recognising and rewarding excellence:** *I hope those warriors who are excellent strong, skilled in*

warfare, whose excellent actions were seen before and the most courageous ones are duly honoured and respected by you.

- **Prompt remuneration:** *I hope you are regularly giving your army the daily provisions and the suitable salary to them, without any delay. When there is delay in giving bread and wages, the servants become incensed against their master and become corrupt; and that is said to be a great unfortunate occurrence.*
- **Handling misconduct:** *He, who does not slay a physician desiring to aggravate the disease, a servant intent on bringing disgrace and a valiant warrior seeking kingly power, is himself slain by them.*

Talent Identification

A leader is only as effective as the people he surrounds himself with because they act as his hands and legs for executing the vision. A story from the Panchatantra shows how careful a leader must be while recruiting people:

Once upon a time, there was a king who kept a monkey as a pet. The monkey served the king in whatever way he could. He had a free run of the royal household because he was the king's pet. One hot day, the monkey sat fanning by the side of the king who was sleeping. He noticed a fly on the chest of the king and tried to swish it away. The fly would go away for the moment and come back again to sit on the king's chest.

The monkey could take it no longer and decided to teach the fly a lesson. He looked for a dagger to kill it and when he found it brought it down with full force on the fly. The fly flew away but the king died as result of the dagger thrust by the monkey.

Moral of the Story: A leader should be careful about the people he keeps around him. Such monkey-like followers may end up doing more harm than good, even if they have the best intentions.

Training in Skills and Values

Training can be understood as the process of development of competencies in an individual. Competencies are the knowledge, skills and values (behaviours) critical to one's growth as an individual and as a resource within the organisation. Many organisations develop a complete competency dictionary of all the competencies that are required for excelling in various roles or functions within the organisation. Such dictionaries grade particular competencies into different levels and ascertain the level of competency needed for executing a particular role in the organisation. For example, the competency of teamwork could have basic, advanced, pro and expert levels. A new employee would need to rise to the basic level of teamwork, a team leader to the advanced level, a project manager to pro level whereas the general manager should have attained expert level of teamwork. This mapping of the job roles and the levels of competencies lays out a learning journey for the individual as they grow in the organisation.

So how does one impart the required training? As per US Bureau of Economic Analysis, the global spending on employee training was a whopping $366.2 billion. However, researchers have claimed that a significant amount of the spending on training doesn't result in intended results. In the book *Evaluating Training Programs: The Four Levels* (1st Edition, Berrett-Koehler, 1993), Donald Kirkpatrick suggests a different approach to designing training programs. He writes: 'Trainers must begin with desired results and then determine what behavior is needed to accomplish them. Then trainers must determine the attitudes, knowledge, and skills that are necessary to bring about the desired behavior(s). The final challenge is to present the training program in a way that enables the participants not only to learn what they need to know but also to react favorably to the program.'[17]

He proposes that the impact of training should be assessed at four levels:

- **Level 1 – Reaction:** To what degree participants react favourably to the learning event.
- **Level 2 – Learning:** To what degree participants acquire the intended knowledge, skills and attitudes based on their participation in the learning event.
- **Level 3 – Behaviour:** To what degree participants

apply what they have learned during training when they are back on the job.

- **Level 4 – Results:** To what degree targeted outcomes occur, as a result of the learning event(s) and subsequent reinforcement.

He adds that when training programs are designed with such a comprehensive approach, the effectiveness of the program is enhanced significantly.

Delegation of Responsibilities

Training should result in delegation of responsibilities. Delegation is the sharing of authority, responsibility and accountability between two or more people where:

- Authority is the right to make decisions, allocate resources and take action.
- Responsibility is an obligation to make decisions and take action.
- Accountability is having to answer for results.

Why Delegate?

A typical example of delegation is that as the father of a family sees his children grow, he starts taking the backseat and puts his children in the driver's seat. However, if the father is a control freak and continues to dictate terms, even at a later stage in the development of the family, it will lead to unrest in the family. At a certain stage, the father should start drawing his satisfaction from seeing his children take up serious responsibilities and get the credit. This raises the esteem of the children in the eyes of the father and allows the family to become much more successful as a unit.

Drawing a comparison between the Kauravas and the Pandavas, one can see a stark difference in terms of distribution of authority. In the Kaurava camp, power and authority were reserved at the top, from where the commands were being passed down. On the other hand, in the Pandava camp, power and authority were distributed in a cascading fashion, all through the ranks. The Kaurava army had one head of the army at a time appointed by Duryodhana. This head, though supposedly exercising supreme authority over the eleven Akshauhini divisions of the Kaurava army, was ultimately meant to be a puppet in the hands of Duryodhana. Bhishma, Drona, Karna, Shalya and Ashvatthama got to take up this role one after the other, due to the demise of the previous army chief. On the other hand, the Pandavas operated with the model of distributed leadership, aligned by Krishna's advice. Duryodhana didn't trust his gurus—Bhishma and Drona—whereas Arjuna trusted his disciple Satyaki to handle critical responsibilities. The Pandavas had appointed seven commanders for the seven Akshauhini divisons with Bhima as overall commander:

1. Virat (King of Matsya)
2. Drupad (King of Pancala)
3. Sahadeva (King of Magadha)

4. Dhrshtaketu (King of Chedi)
5. Satyaki (Only warrior from Dwaraka)
6. Shikhandi (Prince of Panchala)
7. Dhrshtadhyuma—Commander in Chief

Galvanised by the trust bestowed upon them, these seven commanders fought powerfully and became the cause of the downfall of stalwart Kaurava warriors like Bhishma and Drona.

By delegating duties to subordinates, the leaders can free up their time and mental space to concentrate on critical projects/tasks. The subordinates, on the other hand, can get opportunities to develop job competency and leadership skills. Exposure to fresh challenges keeps them dynamic and motivated and gives them reassurance that their leaders have trust in their abilities. Thus, delegation ensures that future organisational leaders are being prepared while present productivity is also being enhanced.

Despite all these benefits, delegation is not practiced widely and effectively. Some of the typical reasons why people don't delegate are:

- 'I can do the task better myself.'
- 'I can do the task faster myself.'
- 'It will take too much time to explain what I want.'
- 'I enjoy doing this myself.'
- 'This task is so important, how can I trust anyone else to do it?'

- 'I don't want to burden anyone else.'
- 'What if they become better than me and replace me?'
- 'They will get the credit, not me.'

Whom to Delegate to and How Much?

The most important question is how to determine how much to delegate to whom. Two factors need to be considered to ascertain this:

- **Skill:** Are they fully capable of doing the task?
- **Will:** Do they want to do the task?

Ability or skill is not the only factor in the decision on delegation. Ability has to be complemented with willingness to do the task for successful delegation. Here are some thumb rules regarding to whom, what and how much to delegate:

How to Delegate?

There are two styles of delegation: **dictatorial** and **empowering**. Often, leaders delegate specific tasks without transferring significant ownership and authority to the subordinate. They spell out rigid instructions for the subordinates and want them to mechanically run through them without applying their intelligence, making any amends or asking any questions. Such tight control squeezes any inspiration out of the subordinate, making them feel suffocated. Delegation is about releasing control and trusting the ability and diligence of the subordinate.

Delegation Matrix		Trust Skills? YES	Trust Skills? No
Trust Motivation?	Yes	**FULLY DELEGATE:** Give full responsibility for completing the task	**DEVELOP:** Work with team member to complete the task or assign developmental resources
	NO	**MANAGE:** Monitor progress to ensure schedules are met and create inspiration to do the task	**RE-DEPLOY:** Find another task/department to delegate to the individual

Here is a comparison between the dictatorial and empowering styles of delegation:

Dictatorial	*Empowering*
Focused on methods	Focused on results
Delegator is responsible for results	Delegatee is responsible for results
Discourages commitment on the part of the delegatee	Involves mutual commitment of delegator and delegatee
Undermines trust	Based on and building trust
Engages the body	Engages imagination, conscience and free will
Gives no future prospects	Prepares for future responsibility
Self-limiting	Allows growth
System collapses in absence of delegator	The system is sustainable in absence of delegator
Creates peons, 'yes-men', zombies	Perpetuates generations of leaders

Theodore Roosevelt, the 26th US president once said, 'The best executive is the one who has sense enough to pick good men to do what he wants done, and self-restraint enough to keep from meddling with them while they do it.' The leader may just tell them what needs to be done with some guidelines and leave it on the subordinate to use their creativity and figure out how to do it. In a place where honest mistakes are not tolerated, 'playing safe' will be the predominant behavioural pattern and people will never grow and rise to meet fresh challenges. Subordinates develop when:

- Trusted and empowered with authority
- Allowed freedom and opportunity to experiment
- Accepted with tolerance for honest mistakes

LEADERSHIP 101: ACTIVITY 4

Reflect on how delegation is beneficial; and why we are unwilling to delegate.

1. BENEFITS

Brainstorm and list the potential benefits of effective delegation—reasons why leaders should delegate.

2. BARRIERS

Brainstorm and list potential barriers—reasons why leaders are unwilling to delegate.

LEADERSHIP 101: ACTIVITY 5

Say suppose, you have 5 employees deployed to do a particular task in the organisation. In the matrix below, identify the quadrant where each of these employees fall with respect to that task. You can write their names in the respective quadrant.

Task under consideration: ____________________

Delegation Matrix		Trust Skills?	
		YES	No
Trust Motivation?	Yes	FULLY DELEGATE	DEVELOP
	NO	MANAGE	RE-DEPLOY

Succession Planning

Leadership successions are critical junctures in the journey of an organisation. A good succession plan ensures that the organisation doesn't suffer or collapse with movement of people within or outside the organisation. It is the responsibility of a leader to set a succession plan rolling well in time, to give sufficient lead time for the successor to take over smoothly. This concern of a leader is reflected in Dashrath as he is thinking of coronating Rama as the King, 'Will Rama become king while I am still alive? Shall I enjoy that happiness?' (Ramayana, *Ayodhya Kand*, 1.35.)

Succession means to pass on the baton that is carried by a responsible office bearer to an upcoming one. What does this baton represent? What actually is to be passed on from one generation of leaders to the next? The baton represents the mood, message and methods of the predecessor which correspond to thoughts, words and actions. Following are components of mood, message and methods:

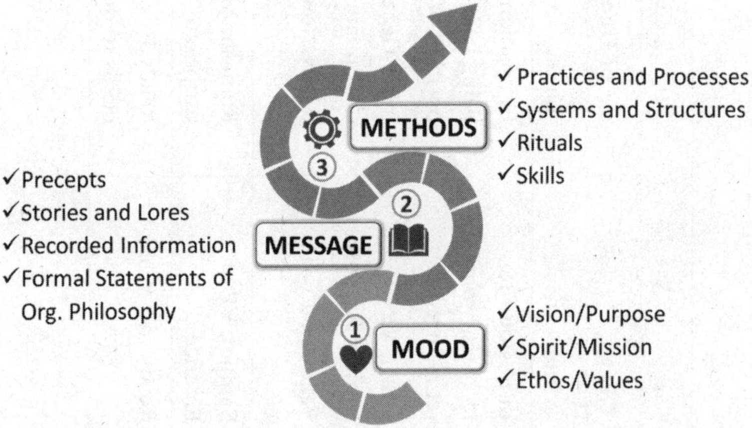

Succession planning entails regularly conducting developmental, support and search activities to ensure that the institution continues effectively when the staff who occupy key roles leave, retire or are elevated to

#	1	2	3
Position	**CEO**	**VP of Human Resources**	**VP of Operations**
Held by	Arthur	Linda	Arnava
Situation	In position for 14 years, wants to retire in 3 years	In position for 5 years, being considered for position of CEO	In position for 8 years, wants to switch
Candidate 1	Linda, VP of Human Resources	John, General Manager of Human Resources	Garry, General Manager of Operations
Developmental Needs	Ready in 2 years	Ready Now	Ready in 2 years
Candidate 2	Samuel, VP of Finance	Ramesh, Manager of Corporate Staffing	Replacement hiring (Search)
Developmental Needs	Ready in 3 years	Ready in 4 years, needs to do an MBA	

higher levels in the organisation. It is different from replacement hiring which is a response to a vacancy. Succession planning is a proactive process that addresses needs before they arise. It is helpful to draw a succession plan for each key role within the organisation. The table on the left page gives an example.

The Organisational Environment—Management Systems

The organisational environment comprises of the organisational hierarchy, reporting relations, policies, regulations and decision-making processes. As previously mentioned, the organisational environment serves as the nervous system of an organisation. It is responsible for synchronised coordination of all the functions and units within the organisation, in order to ensure fulfillment of strategic objectives. In our chariot model of leadership, the organisational environment is represented by the chariot itself which forms the basis and support for everything else. The chariot provides mobility to the warrior, shields him from attacks and serves as a great vantage point for the warrior to take his aim. A good chariot, i.e., organisational environment, thus ensures swift, safe and smooth operations.

Organisation Structure

An organisation gets its organised-ness from the structures and systems built into it. This kind of structure is a system of hierarchy which determines the position and role of every individual in the organisation and their interaction with others. In other words, the organisational structure lays out who does what so the company can meet its objectives. Organisations use a RACI matrix to clearly define the key roles connected

R	Responsible — Person working on activity
A	Accountable — Person with decision authority
C	Consult — Key stakeholder who should be included in decision or work activity
I	Inform — Needs to know of decision or action

to individual tasks. Shri Rama divided his monkey army into battalions with an able leader at the helm and assigned them to attack specific spots of Ravana's fort based on their specific strengths. In other words, Shri Rama created a suitable organisational structure to combat the challenge he had. Here are some details from the *Yuddha Kanda* of the Ramayana:

> At the eastern gate of Lanka, Nila that lion among monkeys for his part, surrounded by many monkeys, should attack Prahasta.
>
> At the southern gate, Angada the son of Vali,

> surrounded by his mighty army, should oppose Mahaparshva and Mahodara.
>
> Let Hanuman, that son of the Wind and of inscrutable spirit, surrounded by a multitude of monkeys, enter the City through the western gate.
>
> With the aid of Lakshmana, I shall forcibly enter the northern gate where Ravana, the one who is oppressing multitudes, is stationed along with his army.
>
> Let the mighty Sugreeva, the king of monkeys, the valiant Jambavan, the king of bears and Vibhishana, the younger brother of the Lord of demons, occupy the central position of the army.

Any medium-to-big-size organisation will have five tiers of leadership, each of which steers a different level of operations of the organisation. The chart on the next page shows these five levels of leadership.

A growing organisation needs to ensure that it has qualified people holding portfolios at all these levels of leadership.

An organisation can be compared to the human body. The human body has a specific shape and various limbs which interact and cooperate with one another as per a pre-ordained design to serve as a whole. The limbs of the organisation are the people who perform various roles just as the liver, heart, brain, etc., perform different functions. The organisation as a whole has a specific shape and chain of command just like the human body has a specific shape and biological work flow.

01	**Visionary Level Leadership**	**Guides Businesses and Creates New Businesses** o Shapes the vision and principles for the organisation and gives the strategic direction o Eg. CEO/Board of Director
02	**Strategic Level Leadership**	**Manages Business and Creates New Business** o Crafts and executes strategic plan in alignment with vision and values , Guides from a distance o Eg. Business Head/Country Head/Key Function Head
03	**Business Level Leadership**	**Manages Business** o Multiple functions converge at Business level, he is responsible for integration & performance of all functions o Eg. Plant/Regional Manager
04	**Managerial Level Leadership**	**Manages People and Operations** o organises people and resources for accomplishing a function/project/operation o Eg. Team Leader/Project or Function Manager
05	**Foundational Level Leadership**	**Manages Self** o Acquires foundational knowledge, skills & values and makes productive contributions through ones talent and skills o Eg. New Entrant/Trainee

This specific shape and chain of command constitutes the organisation structure. It is typically illustrated in some sort of chart or diagram showing the position and roles of different people in the organisation. These structures facilitate orderliness and eliminate confusion, unnecessary conflict and duplication of work.

There are several ways in which organisation structures can be classified. We are presenting only three main types of organisation structures here:

1. Horizontal
2. Vertical
3. Matrix

Horizontal

A horizontal organisation structure is a flat structure, which means that there are very few managers and more authority is granted to rank-and-file employees. This structure is mostly adopted by small companies and startups in their early stages. In the startup environment, everyone knows everyone else and things are directly communicated and coordinated without going through a chain of command. As the size grows, more functional specialization and structural clarity is needed to cope with increased size and complexity. Small companies operate in a personalised, intuitive manner, but as they grow they need to develop more objective, clear and functional ways of fulfilling the organisation's purposes which requires vertical structure. The challenge is to bring about functional differentiation without sacrificing human creativity and commitment.

Vertical

A vertical organisation structure is a pyramidal top-down structure, with a CEO or owner at the top, a middle section of managers and a bottom section of professionals. Three main types of vertical structure exist—**functional, divisional** and **geographical:**

- **Function:** Employees are grouped according to the core function they provide like IT, finance, sales, etc. An advantage of this structure is employees are grouped according to skill set and function, allowing them to focus their collective energies on executing their roles as a department.
- **Geography:** Employees are grouped based on their region like North America, South Asia, Middle East and so on. This structure allows for close communication and collaboration within the geographical region.
- **Division:** If a company is producing multiple products or offering different services it can be grouped according to the product or service like SUV, Sedans, electric cars, etc. This structure provides for autonomy of operation to each division.

Matrix

A matrix structure combines the functional and divisional structures to create a dual command situation. In a matrix structure, an employee reports to two managers—one related to administrative functions like IT, finance, sales, etc., and another corresponding to the business unit related to a product, service, customer or geography. The advantage of this structure is that employees can share their knowledge across the different functional divisions, allowing for better communication and understanding of each function's role. And by working across functions, employees can broaden their skills and knowledge, leading to professional growth within the company.

Strategic Planning

By definition, strategic planning is the method by which an organisation determines how it shall set its best foot forward to meet the challenges and opportunities of the future, ultimately leading to the fulfillment of its vision. For strategic planning to be successful, the organisation's leaders need to spend a significant amount of their current time planning an improved future. That is, they must escape the demands of the day-to-day activities and devote time to working on that improved future.

There is a saying in strategic planning circles: 'A plan that is not written down is not a plan.' But writing down a strategic plan for your project is only the first step. Strategic plans need to be reviewed, updated and adjusted according to time and place. Working on a plan and then not implementing it is a waste of everyone's time. The strategic plan must move from the world of ideas into the world of action. The detailed process of strategic planning and execution has been discussed elaborately in a separate chapter.

Communication

Ben Horowitz, VC at A16Z and author of *The Hard Thing about Hard Things*, says that, 'The CEO's most important operational responsibility is designing and implementing the communication architecture for the company. Absent a well-designed communication architecture, information and ideas will stagnate and your company will become a bad place to work at.'

Building a communication protocol minimises communication gaps and ensures alignment at all levels. A communication protocol is a formal process that outlines the types of information to be communicated within the organisation, as well as identifying the person(s) responsible for communicating particular topics. The protocol also outlines the audience, frequency and suggested vehicles for each type of communication. The following table is a typical format for communication protocols:

#	Message	Who Delivers	Venue/Vehicle	Audience	Frequency
1	Strategic Plan	CEO	E-mail	All	Monthly, Quarterly, Annually
2	Market Updates	Market/Service Leaders	Zoom Call	Market/Service Practitioners	Quarterly
3	Project News and Updates	Project Managers	Zoom/Conference Room	Project Team	Weekly

LEADERSHIP 101: ACTIVITY 6

We had mentioned that an organisation is composed of operational, people and managerial systems. Rate your organisation as to the efficacy of each of these three systems and mention things you would like to work on based on the contents of the book:

The Physical Environment—Operational Systems

#	Components	Rating (1 to 5)	Things to work on
1	Process approach and standardisation		
2	Innovation and continuous improvement		
3	Execution		

The Social Environment—People Systems

#	Components	Rating (1 to 5)	Things to work on
1	Organisational culture		
2	Training and delegation		
3	Succession		

The Organisational Environment—Management Systems

#	Components	Rating (1 to 5)	Things to work on
1	Organisation structure		
2	Strategic planning		
3	Communication		

6. MEETING FACILITATION

Let the Brains Deal with the Storm,
Rather than Create Another

Meetings are like the rudder which helps steer the team or organisation in the desired direction and are therefore crucial for its success. However, if meetings are not organised properly, they can be counter-productive, not only resulting in wastage of valuable time but may also lead to schisms in the team due to misunderstandings and conflicts. In a study of time budgeting at large corporations, Bain & Company found that a single weekly meeting of midlevel managers was costing an organisation $15 million a year. It is said that a middle manager is likely to spend about 35% of time in meetings while someone in upper management may spend a whopping 50% of time in meetings. Meetings that proceed without an agenda, direction or conclusions, result in a cumulative waste of time of all the attendees. Bill Gates writes in his book, *Business at the Speed of Thought*, 'Those meetings that are planned well in advance are the most effective ones.' It is therefore essential to plan meetings properly so that valuable time and energy is directed effectively.

A lot of wisdom on meeting facilitation can be gathered from the system of gram panchayat in India. Gram panchayat are essentially self-governing assemblies or councils which looks after all the affairs of the village. The panchayat represents not only the collective will, but also the collective wisdom of the entire rural community. The *Bhagavata Purana* gives us an account of one such gram panchayat of the village of Gokul where Lord Krishna used to stay in his childhood. Gokul is a community of cowherds whose livelihood comes from milking of cows and from agriculture. The council members of the village of Gokul have assembled to address a serious concern—the village has been repeatedly attacked by terrorists sent by the cruel king, Kamsa. I will quote verses from this section of the *Srimad Bhagavatam* and present some lessons we can derive on meeting facilitation:

gopa-vrddha mahotpatan
anubhuya brhadvane
nandadayah samagamya
vraja-karyam amantrayan

Then one time, having seen the great disturbances (attacks by Kamsas men) in Gokul, all the elderly persons among the cowherd men, headed by Nanda Maharaja, assembled and began to consider what to do to stop the continuous disturbing situations in Vraja.
SB 10.11.21

This verse gives a lot of wisdom about setting up a meeting:

- Agenda of the meeting was clearly defined, which was dealing with disturbances caused by

demons sent by the atrocious King Kamsa to Gokul.
- Relevant stakeholders were invited: Senior members of the gram panchayat of Gokul along with the leaders such as Nanda had assembled.
- An environment conducive for open and honest discussions was created: Everyone had an opportunity to put forward their views.
- Discussion was solution oriented rather than problem oriented.

tatropananda-namaha
gopo jnana-vayo-'dhikah
desa-kalartha-tattva-jnah
priya-krd rama-krishnayoh

At this meeting of all the inhabitants of Gokula, a cowherd man named Upananda, who was the most mature in age and knowledge and was very experienced according to time, circumstances and country, made this suggestion for the benefit of Rama and Krishna.

SB 10.11.22

One of elder members of the panchayat, Upananda was chosen as the facilitator of this meeting. This verse gives the qualifications of a meeting facilitator:

- **Knowledge:** Knowledge involves heoretical and technical knowhow.
- **Experience:** On groundwork experience at the grassroot level, Upananda was not only learned

but also had practical knowledge of leading a cowherd community.

- **Wisdom:** This concerns applying knowledge and experience as per time, place and circumstances. Knowledge and experience can help one solve routine or repetitive problems but when situations become complex, you need someone with wisdom to resolve the complexities.
- **Benevolence:** Proven commitment to work for the good of the organisation

Upananda puts forward a proposal that the entire cowherd community relocate to a new place called Vrindavan which is safer and is more lucrative for their agrarian economy. He concludes by giving a call for action:

tat tatradyaiva yasyamah
sakatan yunkta ma ciram
godhanany agrato yantu
bhavatam yadi rocate

Therefore, let us immediately go today. There is no need to wait any further. If you agree to my proposal, let us prepare all the bullock carts and put the cows in front of us, and let us go there.

SB 10.11.29

We can learn some principles about placing a proposal to the group from the above:

- Any proposal should stand on strength of sufficient logical reasoning and historical evidence. (Upananda presents a lot of reasoning and evidence before presenting his conclusion here).

- Any proposal put forward shouldn't be imposed—it should be opened for discussion and debate and only after a consensus emerges, it may be executed.
- Plan of execution should also be submitted along with the proposal, so that it becomes immediately actionable.

The proposal was unanimously approved by all the cowherd men in the assembly:

tac chrutvaika-dhiyo gopah
sadhu sadhv iti vadinah
vrajan svan svan samayujya
yayu rudha-paricchadah

Upon hearing this advice from Upananda, the cowherd men unanimously agreed. 'Very nice,' they said, 'Very nice.' Thus they sorted out their household affairs, placed their clothing and other paraphernalia on the carts, and immediately started for Våndavana.

SB 10.11.30

Thus, we see that a unanimous consensus emerged through the meeting and the cowherd community immediately decided to relocate to a safer and more lucrative place.

Based on the above passage, I shall be sharing five

principles of meeting facilitation which can help make your meetings lean and effective:

1. **Formulation:** Articulation and Communication of Purpose and Agenda
2. **Navigation:** Steering the Meeting Effectively
3. **Participation:** Ensuring Open Dialogue and Involvement
4. **Resolution:** Arriving at Consensus and Conclusions
5. **Action and Evaluation:** Ensuring Implementation

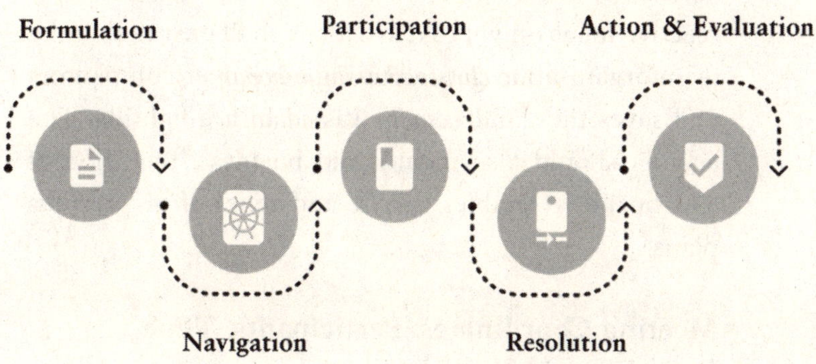

FORMULATION—ARTICULATION AND COMMUNICATION OF AGENDA

Scope of the Meeting: Agenda/List of Topics to be Covered

The purpose of the meeting will determine the scope, agenda and participants of the meeting. It should be defined and an agenda drawn based on it. A meeting agenda is a list of items that participants hope to accomplish at a meeting. It defines boundaries that the meeting must adhere too.

Generally, a meeting agenda should include both reactive and proactive items. A reactive meeting is held to fire-fight changes in the environment, internal or external. Reactive agendas deal with various measures to deal with the problems already at hand. A proactive agenda helps identify future opportunities and challenges and draft a plan to address them. The agenda of meetings should not always come with a reactive focus only. Proactive focus shall ensure that the team/organisation gets a cutting edge over competitors and saves time and energy wasted in fire-fighting. The agenda should also include old business. Inclusion of 'old business' enables review and renewal of previous plans.

Meeting Coordinates: Participants, Time, Duration and Venue

A list of relevant stakeholders is drawn up as participants of the meeting based on the agenda. The length of the meeting also depends on the agenda. One way to keep people focused on the agenda is to keep the meeting as short as possible. Time and venue are important considerations for facilitating the participation of intended participants.

Notice of the Meeting: Circulate Agenda in Advance

Agenda must be circulated in advance (minimum 24 hours) to give the participants enough time to prepare. Relevant documents should be attached to the meeting notice and agenda when you distribute them to the invited participants.

NAVIGATION—STEERING THE MEETING

Every meeting should have a meeting facilitator or chairman who steers the proceedings. Some leaders delegate meeting facilitation to others so that their weight doesn't dominate the proceedings and an open discussion is ensured. Without being steered properly, the conversations in team meetings can go all over the place. So, it is important to do a lot of framing at the beginning and throughout any meeting. Placement can cover how long the meeting will go for, the goal of the meeting, everybody's role in the meeting, type of conversation that needs to happen (e.g., brainstorming, goal setting, and the like), any agreements made earlier about the meeting, follow-up items from previous meetings, and so on.

Consensus on Meeting Agenda

At the beginning of the meeting, the facilitator may check with the participants if they have the same understanding of the meeting goals. Any suggestions for addition or modification in the agenda can be considered by the group for being included in the current meeting/for being resolved separately in person or over email/scheduling the same for the next meeting. But once the agenda is clear to everyone, there should be a general understanding and commitment to stick to the agreed agenda.

Managing the Conversation

The facilitator ensures that there is active and effective participation by all members. Not that everyone speaks equally on every topic but that if anyone has something valuable to contribute on a particular subject, they should get a chance and not get thwarted or eclipsed by others who are very vocal. The facilitator's role is to ensure that the discussion is not unduly dominated by any particular person/s or hijacked by a particular contentious point. If the facilitator sees that the discussion on a particular subject is spiralling in an unproductive way, they should intervene and refocus the conversation to the larger agenda.

Discussing problems requires less commitment than discussing solutions. A leader gently steers the team toward a more useful direction, such as focusing on solutions and then letting them do the thinking. As the chairperson of the meeting, the leader would also need to clarify and summarise the discussion intermittently. This helps bring a complex set of ideas to a conclusion by simplifying the conversation to the bottom line. This also helps raise the conversation to the next level.

Time Management

Fixed starting and ending times evoke focus, seriousness and trust of the group. Ideally, there should be time estimates for all the items on the agenda and if one of items needs to be discussed in even more depth, a separate meeting can be arranged which zeros in on that topic.

PARTICIPATION—ENSURING OPEN DIALOGUE AND INVOLVEMENT

James Detert, a professor at Cornell's Johnson Graduate School of Management, says 'We have a deep set of defense mechanisms that make us careful around people in authority positions.' The role of a facilitator is to create an environment of trust, accommodativeness and creative thinking. Following are some factors which thwart people from openly sharing their ideas and opinions:

- If they feel they will be judged or persecuted for holding a particular opinion
- If people think the outcome is pre-determined and their suggestion will be redundant or inconsequential
- If people are often snubbed or interrupted in the middle of their speech
- If the price of sharing an idea is the responsibility to execute it, people may think twice before sharing

You can consider brainstorming the round-robin method to facilitate contribution by all members. This method allows team members to generate ideas without being influenced by any one person. Another advantage of this approach is that it also ensures that all the members get an equal chance to present their ideas. In the Ramayana, the decision regarding accepting Ravana's brother, Vibhishana, in Shri Rama's camp is a very crucial one. Shri Rama invites opinions of all the monkey generals one by one to help arrive at the decision, 'An efficient and intelligent person ever desirous of everlasting well-being of his friends should properly advise them well in difficult matters. Hence, tell your opinion one by one as to whether I should accept Vibhishana as part of our camp.'

RESOLUTION—ARRIVING AT CONCLUSIONS

At the end of the discussion on each agenda item, the facilitator summarises the discussion and spells out the decisions and action items. Also, at the end of the meeting, a summary of the entire discussion is presented with key decision and action items. This helps bring clarity and commitment of the group for the resolutions of the meeting.

Every discussion item in the meeting could be classified as an action item, a decision or an information. An action item (A) is a to-do assigned to a person/group for completion by a certain date. A decision (D) is a decision or conclusion arrived at by the group during

the meeting. Information (I) is a piece of information shared during the meeting which could be useful as a reference for future.

Following is a good format for capturing the proceedings of the meeting:

Meeting regarding: ____________ **Date:** _/_/ ___
Attendees: ______________________________

Abbreviations used: A: Action, D: Decision, I: Information

S.NO.	MOM	A/D/I	By Whom	By When
1	**Agenda 1**			
1.1	Point 1	I		
1.2	Point 2	A	...	...
1.3	Point 3	D		
2	**Agenda 2**			
2.1	Point 1	A	...	...
2.2	Point 2	A	...	...
3	**Agenda 3**			
3.1	Point 1	D		
3.2	Point 2	A	...	...
3.3	Point 3	A	...	...

ACTION AND EVALUATION—ENSURING IMPLEMENTATION

If the decisions taken during the meeting are not acted upon, the whole meeting can be a waste of time. It is therefore very essential to capture all the decisions and action items decided during the meeting and keep following up on the execution of the decisions. The role of an executive secretary is very important for ensuring effectiveness of the plans drawn up in the meeting. The executive secretary captures the proceedings of the meeting and follows up with the participants on the fulfillment of their commitments after the meeting. Following are some of the responsibilities of the executive secretary:

1. *Before the meeting:*
   - Sends out invitation of the meeting and circulates the agenda well in advance
   - Ensures availability of the venue and the amenities for the meeting
   - Ensures that all the information, documents, powerpoints, printouts, etc., required for the meeting are kept ready

2. *During the meeting:*
   - Takes notes of the proceedings
   - Keeps track of decisions
   - Keeps track of action items: who does what by when

3. *After the meeting:*
    - Shares relevant documents with the individuals/group on email, etc.
    - Prompts people about upcoming deadlines
    - Follows up with the participants on what they agreed to do
    - Helps schedule next meeting based on the availability of participants

Thus, we have presented five essential principles for conducting effective meetings. Hopefully these will help you get good returns on the investment of time and energy in your meetings.

7. STRATEGIC PLANNING AND EXECUTION

Aim for the Sky with Feet on the Ground

A plan without action is a daydream whereas action without a plan in place is a nightmare. Without proper planning, execution may be ineffective and even disastrous. On the other hand, good execution can take a simple idea and turn it into profitable, successful business. Bad execution, however, can ruin a brilliant idea and turn it into a pile of debts and a bunch of burnt-out people. Ram Charan, co-author of *Execution: The Discipline of Getting Things Done*, states, 'Seventy percent of strategic failures are due to poor execution. It is rarely for lack of smarts or vision.' Thus, planning and execution go hand in hand.

You will find research papers and articles elaborately discussing the process of drafting a strategic plan while barely touching upon execution. You will also find papers on how to do cutting-edge execution while minimally touching upon the process of strategic planning. Here we shall share with you a simple seven-step process which seamlessly integrates strategic planning and execution so that you can develop a great strategic plan and translate that into reality through rigorous execution:

1. **Ideate:** clear and inspiring vision
2. **Formulate:** action plan
3. **Communicate:** alignment and synergy of vision and goals
4. **Incubate:** favourable environment and work culture
5. **Collaborate:** creative co-operation and discipline
6. **Facilitate:** problem solving and resource allocation
7. **Evaluate:** assessment and accountability

While explaining these steps, we shall also depict episodes from the Ramayana which highlight important aspects of strategic planning. Shri Rama, in the form of a human, with an army of monkeys and bears was able to defeat Ravana, a demon with incredible mystic powers and an army of well-known warriors, because of right strategy formulation and implementation. Shri Rama's triumph, apart from having followed the path

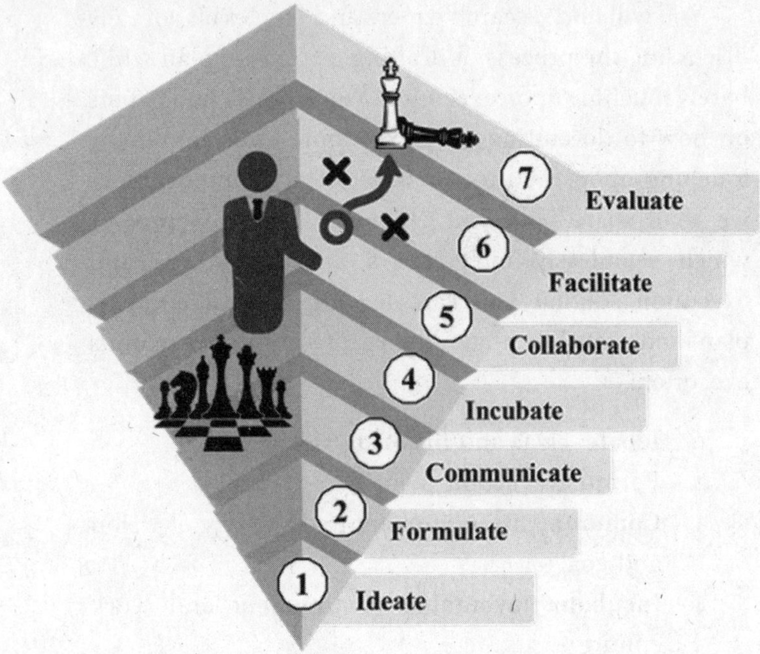

of righteousness and ethics, also comes from following a right strategic management process highlighted in various episodes across the Ramayana. An example of choosing the best strategy amongst possible alternatives is demonstrated by Hanuman as he mulls over the best way he can break into the ranks of the demons of Lanka and thus be able to spy about their strengths: 'In the case of demons, the strategy of negotiation is not practicable as they are arrogant. For the rich residents of the golden Lanka having abundant wealth, the strategy of bribery is not suitable. For persons who are proud of their strength, as in the case of these demons, the strategy of sowing dissension is not amenable. Prowess alone is agreeable for me here.' After meeting Mother Sita, Hanuman had four alternatives available to him to know the strength of the demons at Lanka. They were sowing dissension, negotiation, bribery and open assault; he chose the fourth strategy of open assault.

SEVEN-STEP STRATEGIC PLANNING PROCESS

Ideate: Clear and Inspiring Vision

French aviator and author of the early 20th century, Antoine De Saint-Exupery's perspective of the importance of ideas is, 'Rocks cease to be a pile of rocks when somebody contemplates on them with the idea of a cathedral in mind.' Ideas can and do change the world. It all begins with a dream, a cherished aspiration, a compelling purpose, an idea that doesn't let you sleep. Former Indian President and Space Scientist, A.P.J. Abdul Kalam has famously said, 'Dream is not the thing you see in sleep but is that thing that doesn't let you sleep.' The process of strategic planning begins with identifying that purpose/vision/idea which won't let you sleep. In a more conventional sense, it defines you/your organisation and propels you to do whatever is needed to fulfill it. If the organisation is not clear about their purpose and identity, they can potentially get swayed in so many directions. There is a saying, 'If you don't stand for anything, you are susceptible to fall for everything.' Reflecting on the following questions can help your organisation articulate its vision:

- Who we are?
- Why do we exist?
- What do we stand for?
- What is our purpose?
- What do we value the most?

Based on answers to the above questions, draft a vision statement which encapsulates that compelling and inspiring purpose in a concise form. The Oxford Dictionary defines vision as 'the ability to think about the future with imagination or wisdom'. The vision statement can be thought of as a visualisation of what the organisation wants to do and where it wants to be. It serves as the anchor which gives steady identity and meaning, the polestar which gives direction and the favourable winds which give inspiration to the ship of your organisation.

In the *Srimad Bhagavat Purana*, Lord Krishna states that those who have clear understanding of their vision prosper while others perish:

jnatvajnatva ca karmani
jano 'yam anutisthati
vidusah karma-siddhih syad
yatha naviduso bhavet

When people in this world perform activities, sometimes they understand why they are doing what they are doing and sometimes they don't. Those who know the why achieve success in their work, whereas others do not.

SB 10.24.6

Following are some characteristics of a good vision statement:

- Should be concise and lucid, i.e., neither too verbose nor vague
- Should neither be too broad nor too narrow
- Should be written in the present tense, with a sense of immediacy

Here are examples of vision statements of some successful organisations:

Organisation	***Vision Statement***
Disney	To make people happy.
Microsoft	Empower every person and every organisation on the planet to achieve more.
Nike	Bring inspiration and innovation to every athlete* in the world. (*If you have a body, you are an athlete.)
Oxfam	A just world without poverty.
Smithsonian Museum	Shaping the future by preserving our heritage, discovering new knowledge and sharing our resources with the world.
WWF	We seek to save a planet, a world of life. Reconciling the needs of human beings and the needs of others that share the Earth.

Creative Commons	Nothing less than realising the full potential of the Internet—universal access to research and education, full participation in culture—to drive a new era of development, growth and productivity.

You can also write a list of values which represent your organisation.

FORMULATE: ACTION PLAN

The hallowed vision statement shall fade into oblivion as it hangs on a plaque in your office, unless it is translated into an action plan. In order to formulate a foolproof action plan, one needs to run through a series of steps as depicted in the figure below and explained further:

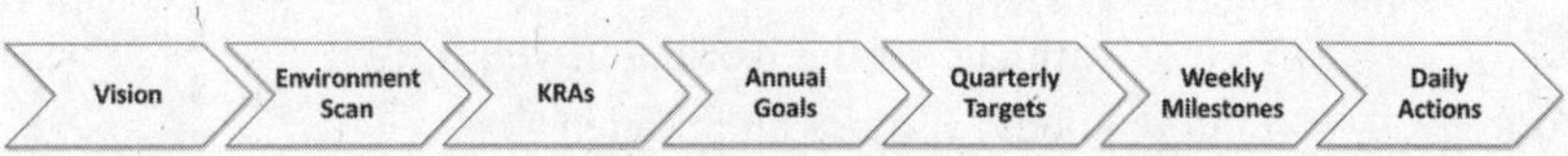

Environmental Scan

Every organisation has an internal and external environment. The external environment comprises of the markets, customers, competitors, technology, socio-political trends, etc. The internal environment comprises of the management systems, operational systems and human and technological resources of the organisation. In the wake of constant changes in these environments, it is important that the organisation scans them regularly to assess its existing strategies and formulate new strategies.

One may particularly look for trends, landmark events, disruptive changes and critical issues while scanning the internal and external environments to ascertain their impact. Based on the scan, the organisation can develop a SWOT (strengths and weaknesses, opportunities and threats) chart. Opportunities and threats are related to the external environment while strengths and weaknesses are related to the internal environment. The SWOT analysis helps understand and minimise the risks and threats and helps the organisation focus on the opportunities which are aligned with its strength. The following chart explains the four elements of SWOT analysis:

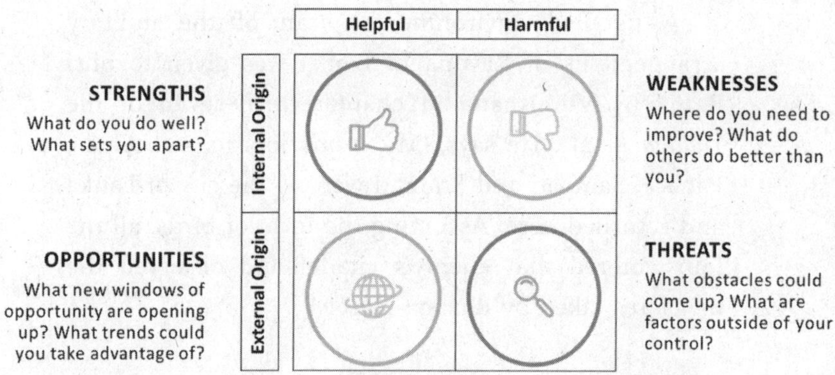

Before finding and meeting Mother Sita, Sri Hanuman went around Lanka and performed an environmental scan of Lanka (Ramayana, *Sundar Kanda*, 4.10). He scanned all the fortifications and highways, armies and spies, palaces and residents. After meeting Mother Sita, Hanuman decided to further examine the strength of the demons in Lanka. His thinking is depicted in the following verse (Ramayana, *Sundar Kanda*, 41.5):

'Then meeting Ravana with his troop of ministers, his army and his followers in battle as well as knowing his designs and strength, I will go back from here happily.' Thus thinking, Hanuman went on a rampage of Lanka and as per his plan, got arrested and was summoned before Ravana. This audience with Ravana and his army chiefs helped Hanuman get a clear picture of Lanka's strengths and weaknesses.

A detailed environmental scan of the military arrangements of Ravana in Lanka was given to Shri Rama by Vibhishana in chapter thirty-seven of the *Yuddha Kanda*. He says, 'My counselors named Anala, Panasa, Sampati and Pramati went to the city of Lanka and returned here. Assuming the form of birds, all the four entered that enemy's citadel and observed the measures taken by Ravana closely.

> O, Rama! I give a detailed report as it was given to me of the defence-arrangements made by the evil-minded Ravana, hear me. The very strong

Prashata is standing near the eastern gate. Mahaparshva and Mahodara of mighty prowess are at the southern gate. Indrajit, the son of Ravana is at the western gate along with many demons armed with harpoons, swords, bows, spears and hammers together with warriors furnished with weapons of various kinds. A prey to great anxiety, Ravana, knower of magical formulas, is himself stationed at the northern gate, along with several thousands of demons holding lances in their hand. As for Virupaksha he with mighty army carrying spears, clubs and bows along with other demons, occupies the center of the fort. The elephants and chariots number some ten thousand each, the cavalry twenty thousand and there are more than a crore foot soldiers. These strong and intrepid demons endeavouring to kill someone in battle have ever been their sovereign's favourites. O, Rama! In these demons, a retinue of ten lacs each is near at hand for each demon. O, Rama! When Ravana attacked Kubera in battle, sixty lac demons sallied forth with him. All of them were akin to the evil-minded Ravana in prowess, in strength, in courage and in pride. Indignation need not be resorted to (by you) based on this report. I am not terrifying you, but only arousing your wrath. You are indeed capable of overpowering even celestials by your valour.

Key Result Areas (KRAs)

Based on the SWOT analysis developed in the environmental scan stage, the organisation can identify the key result areas (KRAs) where it should focus on. KRAs are those critical areas which if focused on can help realise the vision most effectively. The vision or purpose statement is like the destination, values are like a compass for decision making and KRAs are like the map which chart out the journey. KRAs could be identified with respect to the market segment, customer segment, product and the like, where the organisation enjoys competitive advantage or an edge over others. While inquiring from Bharat about the welfare of Ayodhya, Shri Rama speaks about the importance of choosing the right KRA, 'O, Bharata! I hope considering your interest (vision and mission) fully, you launch an undertaking (KRA), which has maximum benefit with minimum cost (competitive advantage) and indeed do not delay it further.' One needs to eliminate alternatives which may not be effective approaches in helping realise the vision.

Apple's transformation is a case of the role of effective KRAs in attaining success. When Steve Jobs returned to Apple in 1997, he had a daunting mission ahead of him. The company had lost $1.04 billion in the fiscal year of 1997. Sales had plummeted by 30% in the last quarter of 1996. On the product line, it was producing a random array of computers and peripherals, including multiple versions of the same product.

After a few weeks of product review sessions, Jobs had had enough. At a product meeting, he decided to reduce the number of products by 70%. Apple was to produce only four products: one desktop and one portable device aimed at both consumers and professionals. The job of his team members was to focus on building four great products, one for each quadrant. All other products were to be cancelled. There was a stunned silence. He relentlessly filtered out what he considered distractions. His move to a smaller product line and a greater focus on quality and innovation paid off. One year later, the company turned a $309 million profit. Jobs identified Apple's KRAs and made the company focus on them exclusively.

Mark Parker, the CEO of Nike, asked Steve if he had any advice. Jobs replied in a similar fashion: 'Well, just one thing ... Nike makes some of the best products in the world. Products that you lust after. But you also make a lot of crap. Just get rid of the crappy stuff and focus on the good stuff.'

The KRAs should be identified with a balanced view of long-term and short-term gains in mind. A short-sighted strategy could prove to be disastrous as it could lack in long-term vision of consequences. A story from the Panchatantra teaches us how:

A big banyan tree was home to a number of cranes in a forest. In the hollow of that tree lived a cobra, which used to feed on the young cranes that had not yet learned to fly. When the mother crane saw the cobra killing her offspring, she began crying. Seeing the sorrowful crane, a crab asked her what made her cry.

The crane told the crab, 'Every day, the cobra living in this tree is killing my children. I am not able to contain my grief. Please show me some way to get rid of this cobra.'

The crab then thought, 'These cranes are our born enemies. I shall give her advice that is misleading and suicidal. That will see the end of all these cranes.'

Then the crab told the crane, 'Strew pieces of meat from the mongoose's burrow to the hollow of the cobra. The mongoose will follow the trail of meat to the cobra burrow and will kill it.'

The crane did as the crab advised her. The strategy worked perfectly fine initially as the mongoose came following the meat trail and killed the cobra. However, as a result, the hungry mongoose came across a good source of food supply in the form of the cranes. He started killing them and ultimately the cranes had to abandon the tree. That is why one needs to have a long-term perspective to be able to foresee what one's strategy would eventually lead to.

Goals

The specific job to be done for each KRA is identified by setting a goal or a set of goals. These goals constitute the key outcomes which, if accomplished, shall help fulfill the vision. Each goal should be associated with a concrete criteria for measuring progress towards the attainment of that goal. In other words, you need to identify both lead and lag measures for your goal. Lag measures are those indices which capture the fulfillment of the goal. Lead measures track the critical activities that drive or lead to the fulfillment of the goal. They predict success of the lag measure. In other words, lag measures will tell you whether you were able to achieve the goal whereas lead measures will help you predict whether you will be able to achieve that goal. For example, for sales of a product online, number of units sold in the quarter are the lag measure whereas number of visitors to the webpage every day or the review rating of the product would act as the lead measure.

The team leader facilitates a collaborative process to create the goals and ensures that everyone is aligned with these goals. In order to be effective, goals should also be **SMART**.

COMMUNICATE: ALIGNMENT AND SYNERGY OF VISION AND GOALS

American author and management consultant, James C. Collins says, 'Building a visionary company requires 1% vision and 99% alignment.' The most compelling vision and foolproof plans shall simply remain the brainchild of a brilliant mind unless the team members/subordinates subscribe to and are aligned with the same ideas. The interesting statistic below shows that, in absence of

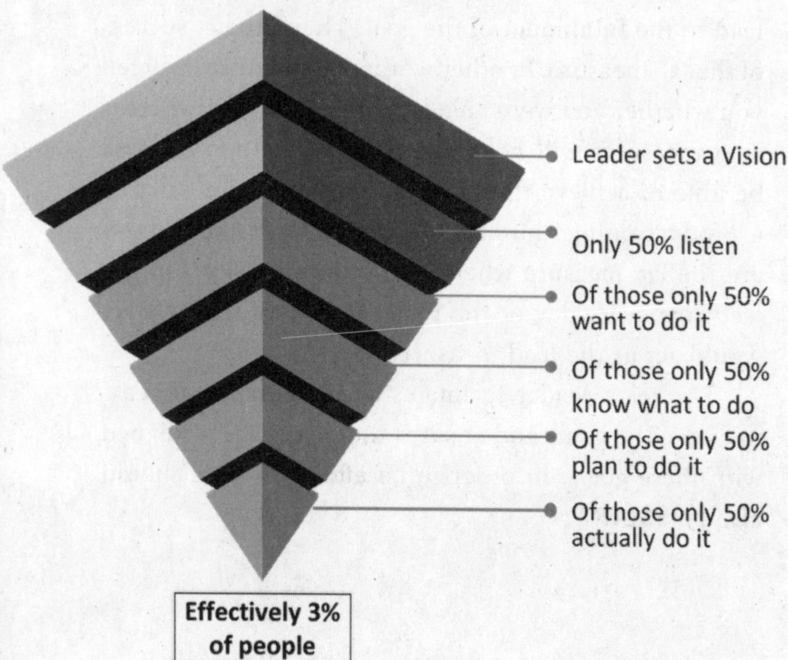

Vision Funnel

good communication, when the leader sets the vision only very few ultimately are tuned in, to work towards fulfilling that vision.

Strategy and execution cannot operate in isolation. They are like intertwined strands of a rope. If strategy formulation is done as an abstract job at the high rungs while the entire rank and file are not involved and not in sync, it will only lead to chaos and confusion. Therefore, it is very essential that the leader is always in dialogue and in sync with their team on all important strategy decisions.

The vision and action plan should be deliberated upon and formulated by the key stakeholders. But later on, efforts should be put to ensure that all concerned stakeholders understand and appreciate the vision and action plan. While inquiring about the welfare of Ayodhya, Shri Rama instructs Bharat about the importance of consulting with the ministers while drafting any major proposals, 'The source of victory for kings indeed comes from a concealed counsel by ministers, who are well-versed in political sciences. I hope that you do not deliberate alone nor indeed with numerous men. I hope that you consult with three or four ministers as mentioned in scriptures any proposal collectively and singly with each of them in person.' (Ramayana 2.100)

INCUBATE: FAVOURABLE ENVIRONMENT AND WORK CULTURE

A good harvest can be reaped from a good soil. A strategic plan is like a good seed but for that seed to germinate and give good harvest, you also need the soil of good environment comprising of organisational culture and work ethics. Without a conducive environment, all efforts in strategic planning will simply increase the stack of papers without translating into any results. Organisational culture consists of the norms, values, beliefs, expectations, behaviours and assumptions that exist within the organisation. A detailed essay on organisational culture has been presented in the chapter 'Leadership 101'. Please refer to it for more details.

COLLABORATE: CREATIVE CO-OPERATION AND DISCIPLINE

All the steps which we have discussed so far are preparatory steps. Their execution happens at this stage, i.e., through discipline and creative cooperation. Chanakya talks about a four-level approach to execution:

'The leader should bring about the commencement of what is not done, the carrying out of what is commenced, the improvement of what is being carried out and the excellence of the execution of orders, in the case of works,' (*Arthashastra* 1.15.51).

In other words, a leader shouldn't become complacent until he sees all the plans translated into reality and even then, endeavour to perfect one's creation. Discipline is the bridge which connects dreams and reality. The power of discipline is often undermined in a world which focuses on skills and talents. In one sense, execution is all about discipline. It takes incredible discipline on part of the organisation to execute its strategic plans. But it takes even more discipline to do so over and over again. Success is only achieved by consistent performance and this consistency is brought about by the practice of discipline. American entrepreneur and author, Jim Rohn, says, 'Success is nothing more than a few simple disciplines, practiced everyday.'

The second important factor in execution is a spirit of creative cooperation. Concerted team effort can accomplish monumental tasks. Take for example Shri Rama's monkey army building a bridge across the ocean. The following is an episode from the Ramayana demonstrating the exceptional teamwork and coordination among the monkeys:

Shri Rama appointed Nala as the chief architect of the bridge, which would have a length of 800 kilometres. Hundreds and thousands of monkey heroes sent by Rama jumped in joy on all sides towards the great forest. Those army-chiefs of monkeys who resembled mountains, broke the rocks and trees there and dragged them away towards the sea. The monkeys filled the ocean with all types of trees—some with roots intact and some others without roots. The huge monkeys with mighty strength uprooted elephant-sized rocks and mountains and transported them by mechanical contrivances. The water, raised due to sudden throwing of mountains in the sea, sored upward towards the sky and from there again, gushed back. The rocks falling on all sides perturbed the ocean. Some others drew up strings a hundred *yojanas* long in order to keep the rocks in a straight line. Nala, on his part, initiated a monumental bridge in the middle of the ocean. The bridge was built at that time with the cooperation among the monkeys. Some monkeys were holding poles for measuring the bridge and some others collected the material. Reeds and logs resembling clouds and mountains, brought by hundreds of monkeys, led by the command of Rama, fastened some parts of the bridge. That beautiful bridge constructed by Nala across the ocean, shone brightly like a milky way of stars in the sky.

An important aspect of collaboration in today's world is forging strategic alliances. Organisations having complementary skill sets come together to fulfill their strategic goals. In the process of achieving their individual goals they also create a higher value for their customers. Shri Rama created a win-win alliance with Sugreeva and Vibhishana to team up against the atrocities of Ravana. Eventually, this alliance led to Shri Rama finding Mother Sita, Sugreeva being reinstated as the king of Kishkinda and Vibhishna becoming the righteous king of Lanka after Ravana's death. Similarly, the Mahabharata also demonstrates the power of strategic collaboration. The following table draws a comparison on the strategic alliances of the Kauravas and the Pandavas.

Kauravas	*Pandavas*
▸ Possessed great wealth and armies of their own. ▸ The greatest empire of the time. But not many powerful allies, except from old relations from far off places like Gandhara (Shakuni), Sindhu (Jayadrath) and Kambodia (Camboja-Bhagadutt)	▸ No wealth/armies of their own. But powerful allies all over the country. ▸ Panchala through marriage with Draupadi. ▸ Magadha through marriage of Sahadeva and Vijaya. ▸ Chedi through marriage of Nakula and Karenmayi. ▸ Kasi through marriage of Bhima and Balandhara. ▸ Kekaya through marriage of Yudhishtira and Devika. ▸ Matsya through marriage of Abhimanyu and Uttara. ▸ Rakshasas through marriage of Bhima and Hidimba. ▸ Nagas through marriage of Arjuna and Uloopi.

FACILITATE: PROBLEM SOLVING AND RESOURCE ALLOCATION

During execution, it may be expected that things won't turn out as per the plan. There might be roadblocks, bottlenecks, delays, resource crunches, vendor issues, quality control issues, talent gaps, communication gaps, conflicts, environmental changes, etc. It is the responsibility of the leader to step in at such times and fill in for the gaps so that the team keeps moving ahead and doesn't get delayed. In order to facilitate execution, the leader should work on the following:

1. **Maintain a bird's eye view:** This would be possible when the leader delegates powers and responsibilities to subordinates and reserves the role of facilitation for themselves. A well-researched method by which leader can get an uber vision of the organisation is 'Management by Exception'. Management by Exception (MBE) is a style of management that gives employees the responsibility to take decisions and to fulfill work or projects by themselves. Under this system, the manager receives only condensed, summarised and invariable comparative reports covering all the elements, and should have all the exceptions to the past averages or standards pointed out, both the especially good and the especially bad exceptions. This gives them a full view of the progress in a few minutes of time. If an unusual situation or anomaly, which could cause difficulties for the business appears that can't be managed by the employee at his level, the employee then passes the decision on to the next, higher level. Troubleshooting is attempted at that level but if the problem is still found to

linger, it is then escalated to the next higher level. Thus, only those issues which really require the attention of the senior management reach them, freeing them up from other roles and tasks.

2. **Have proactive focus:** Being proactive entails staying alert, anticipating problems, planning in advance, scheduling the work smartly, thinking on your feet and taking action with agility whenever needed.

EVALUATE: ASSESSMENT AND ACCOUNTABILITY

It's imperative, even at the planning stage, to build in systems for evaluating progress when the execution happens, so that appropriate course corrections can be made to keep the project on track. A lack of evaluation often implies only token commitment. The Ramayana informs us that Shri Rama had spies go around the kingdom to inform him about the well-being of the people and flag any important issues which needed to be addressed. Thus, the system of espionage was also used to evaluate whether the welfare policies of the state were being executed properly. In the modern context, we could make use of two tools for effective evaluation and course correction: **team scoreboard** and **accountability meetings.**

A team scoreboard is a tool that enables a team to visually monitor and display current team progress on top priorities and goals. It informs them about what has been done and what needs to be done, in what time period and to what extent, in order for the team to succeed. Without a scoreboard, there is a lot of room for ambiguity.

Accountability is the support structure that helps vision to translate into action. Regular accountability meetings can help the team to report and assess progress and then revise and commit to new plans. Following are periodic accountability meetings which could be conducted:

- **Daily Meetings**
  The leader conducts a 5–7 minute meeting with the key people responsible for executing the plan for the day. It creates purpose and urgency to agree on what needs to be done on that day.
- **Weekly Meetings**
  A weekly meeting is conducted at the start of every new week. It is conducted to review the work done in the past week and to set milestones for the upcoming week.
- **Monthly Meetings**
  Here, the focus is on reviewing and setting targets. The overall business model is reviewed along with short-/medium-term plans. Changes, if any, are discussed and steps are taken to adapt to them.
- **Quarterly Meetings**
  A typical quarterly meeting agenda:

1. Review quarterly key performance indicators (KPIs)
2. Review previous quarter's goals and projects
3. Map out upcoming quarter's goals/projects
4. Review strategy and competitive landscape
5. Review marketing and sales strategy

- **Annual Meetings**
  They are formal in nature and accompanied by a formal report that describes the previous year's activities and its associated costs and benefits. It might even contain a projected statement for the upcoming year.

STRATEGIC PLANNING AND EXECUTION: ACTIVITY 1

Ideate

Reflect on the following questions with respect to your organisation:

- Who we are?
- Why do we exist?
- What do we stand for?
- What is our purpose?
- What do we value the most?

Based on answers to the above questions, draft a vision statement which encapsulates that compelling and inspiring purpose in a concise form:

Formulate

Conduct a SWOT analysis for the organisation and its environment:

Strengths	
Weaknesses	
Opportunities	
Threats	

Based on the SWOT analysis, identify your key result areas (KRAs):

#	**Key Result Areas (KRAs)**
1	
2	
3	
4	
5	

Use the following template to derive the actionable goals for your organisation:

KRAs	Goal Statements	Due Date	Responsible

8. DEALING WITH UNCERTAINTY AND CHANGE

Master the Trapeze Act of Change

We are living in a world of volatility, uncertainty, change and ambiguity, i.e., a VUCA world. New, disruptive technologies are emerging and are transforming the nature of work and ways of working. These times of uncertainty and change are throwing both opportunities and challenges at an unprecedented pace for all the players in the market. In other words, the ability to successfully deal with uncertainty and change is now the most critical capability which allows an organisation to not only survive but also thrive. Leaders need to think clearly and act promptly to help their organisations capitalise on the opportunities and navigate through the challenges. The trapeze act is an appropriate metaphor to help us understand how to deal with uncertainty and change. The act involves acrobatic leaps from one trapeze to another. The real challenge in the trapeze act is when you let go of the current trapeze and make that leap. The clouds of change and uncertainty hang high as you are in the air, not sure of whether you will be able to reach the next trapeze in time and latch on to it.

Reversals, uncertainty and change visit as uninvited guests in everyone's life. The story of 'The Bridge to Nowhere' is quite instructive in this context. We are referring to the Choluteca bridge which is a 484-metre long bridge in Honduras, Central America, in a region notorious for storms and hurricanes. Factoring in the possibility of storms, the bridge was designed to withstand powerful forces of nature and was completed in 1998. Coincidentally the same year, Honduras was hit by Hurricane Mitch, which caused considerable damage to the nation and its infrastructure.

The hurricane left behind a very startling sight. While many other bridges were damaged by the hurricane, the Choluteca bridge survived in near perfect condition. However, everything around the bridge had changed to an unrecognisable degree. The roads on either end of the bridge completely vanished without trace. More interestingly, the Choluteca River (which is several hundred feet wide) had carved itself a new channel during the massive flooding caused by the hurricane. It no longer flowed beneath the bridge, which now spanned over dry ground.

The bridge survived but it was now like an artefact in the middle of nowhere and leading to nowhere. It thus became known as The Bridge to Nowhere. The world is changing at an unprecedented pace in unimagined ways. The Choluteca Bridge may not be serving its purpose as a bridge for transportation, but it stands as an artefact to remind us that if we are not prepared to adapt to change, we may end up being obsolete. While we focus on creating the best solutions for existing problems, we also need to factor in the fact that these problems may themselves become redundant in time. While we focus on building the most sophisticated products or services, we also need to think that the market requirements could evolve.

The Covid-19 pandemic has exposed numerous unnecessary assumptions we have built our businesses and economies upon. To name a few—work from home was an unheard of possibility but it has become a new normal and several companies have been pleasantly surprised to see how cost-effective and efficient this has been; for past few decades, cosmopolitan areas had more or less been the epicenters of GDP contribution but now with migration of labour back to their native areas, a new, decentralised model of economy is taking shape; the role of digital technology in delivery of goods and services has assumed unprecedented significance, etc. This is a good time to reflect on and uncover all such assumptions, so that the businesses we build are not only successful in the present but also sustainable in the future.

AGENTS OF UNCERTAINTY AND CHANGE

Where does uncertainty and change come from? It is important to identify the causes and sources of uncertainty and change before trying to devise measures to deal with them. Uncertainty and change can surface through the following agents:

- **Intrinsic (Originating within)**
    - o System-based
    - o People-based

- **Extrinsic (Originating outside)**
  - Circumstance
  - Calamity
  - Conflict

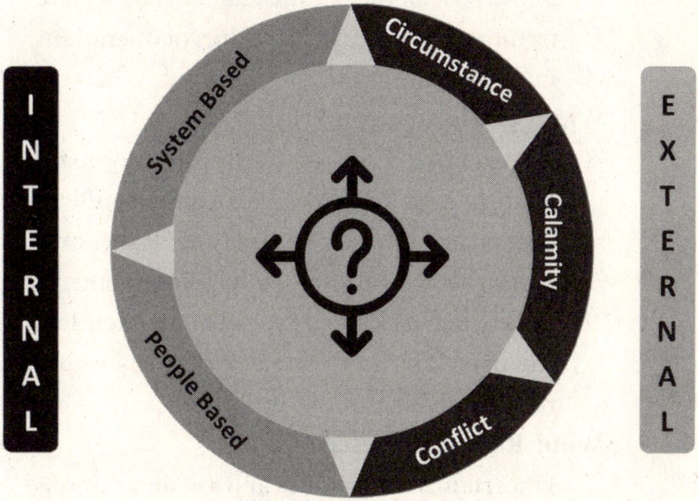

Sources of Uncertainty & Change

System-Based

System-based uncertainties and changes arise because of the following factors:

- **Why? Vision/Purpose**
  - Uncertainty: When the vision of the organisation is not clear or there is ambiguity around it, it results in uncertainty at all levels as vision forms the foundation for everything

else. It may create lot of confusion, conflict and chaos and end up in the formation of splinter groups within the organisation.

- ○ Change: When there is a shift in the vision or purpose of the organisation, it may lead to tremors of change in all realms of operations in the organisation.

- **What? Goals/Strategy/Priority**
  - ○ Uncertainty: Lack of clarity on the goals, strategy and priorities can cause conflicts, friction and unrest. There may be clashes over allocation of resources and disagreements over which tasks ought to get more attention.
  - ○ Change: Change in strategy or goals would require change in the processes.
- **Who? Roles/Job Descriptions**
  - ○ Uncertainty: If the roles and job descriptions aren't clearly defined, you may find instances of duplication of work, poor coordination, confusion, etc., in the organisation.
  - ○ Change: If the roles are swapped or job descriptions are modified/ updated, it needs orientation and knowledge transfer to onboard the people for the new roles/jobs.
- **How? Processes/Systems/Communications/ Technology/Resources/Training**
  - ○ Uncertainty: If the processes and systems aren't well defined and documented, small tasks would end up becoming very

laborious, chances of bureaucracy creeping into the system would increase and people may act whimsically and manipulate things to suit to their convenience or vested interests. If channels of communications aren't properly defined, you may end up with problems of lack of communication or miscommunication. Technological modifications may also lead to uncertainties if proper training is not conducted.

- Change: Changes in processes, systems and technology need proper onboarding. There may be resistance in the staff to these changes as it may mean going up a new learning curve.

- **Where? Work Environment/Organisational Culture**
  - Uncertainty: A disorganised and untidy workplace prevents employees from having clear thought processes and thus reduces the efficiency and satisfaction levels of the staff. Similarly, organisational culture has the potential to draw out the best or the worst from any employee.
  - Change: When people get adapted to a particular work environment or organisational culture, it becomes difficult for them to accept and adapt to a new one.

- **What If? Backup Plan/Crisis Management**
  - Uncertainty: In case of eventualities, if a backup plan or crisis management plan is not in place, it shall create lot of uncertainty and chaos.
  - Change: Changes in backup plans or crisis management plans should be communicated properly, else in times of eventualities, there would be turmoil.

People-Based

- **Leadership:** Leadership is the engine of any organisation. Any changes in the leadership or changes by the leadership are crucial as they are generally accompanied by a dominos effect.
- **Employee Attrition:** The 2016 Deloitte Millennial Survey notes that 44% of millennials say, if given the choice, they would like to leave their current employer in the next two years. The direct cost of replacing an employee depends on their position.[18] For example, replacing a mid-level employee can cost 20% of their annual salary whereas replacing a high-level employee, with large salaries and specialised training, can cost up to 200% of their salary. Indirect costs of employee turnover are intangible and of greater magnitude than direct costs. They can include factors like lost productivity, loss of tacit

knowledge, loss of morale and trust amongst existing employees etc.

- **Team-Synergy/Composition:** Teams are specialised units designed to carry out a particular project or a certain process by mutually complementing each other with their different skill sets. Any disturbance to the delicate composition of the team or a lack of coordination amongst the team members could lead to compromised results and uncertainty. Mutual conflicts within the team could also lead to significant losses.

Circumstance

With time, the ecosystem in which the organisation operates goes through changes and/or evolution. The changes in the environment warrant corresponding adjustments to deal with them so that it doesn't become obsolete or ineffective. Following are some of the changes which occur in the ecosystem:

- **Cultural metamorphosis:** Changes in culture bring about changes in tastes and preferences of the populace. To stay relevant, the organisation must adapt its products and services to suit to the tastes and ethos of the new generation.
- **Technological evolution:** The past century has seen major changes brought about due to the evolution of technology. According to the

World Economic Forum, 'The First Industrial Revolution used water and steam power to mechanize production. The Second used electric power to create mass production. The Third used electronics and information technology to automate production. The Fourth Industrial Revolution is characterized by a fusion of technologies that is blurring the lines between the physical, digital, and biological spheres.' Disruptive technologies have changed the landscape of the markets. Airbnb, the world's largest accommodation provider, actually owns no property. Facebook, the world's largest media company, generates no content. Uber, the world's largest taxi company, owns no cars. Alibaba, the world's highest volume merchant company, owns no inventory. Netflix, the world's largest movie house, owns no cinemas. Companies which have been alert and agile to adapt to the changes in technology have flourished while others have had to perish.

- **Economic meltdown:** The credit crisis of England of 1772 led to the American Revolution. The Great Recession of 2008 due to collapse of the housing bubble in US and that of Lehmann Brothers led to the wiping out of thousands of jobs. Lehman Brothers filed for bankruptcy on 15 September, 2008. With $639 billion in assets, it was the biggest bankruptcy filing in the history.

About 26,000 of the firm's employees worldwide lost their jobs and investors suffered immense losses, fueling the US's greatest economic downturn since the crash of 1929. Economic meltdowns throw every player, big or small, into a level playing field of uncertainty and crisis.

- **Environmental change:** The warming of global climate is now unequivocal. Over the last 100 years (1906–2005), the global temperature has increased by 0.74°C. The global sea level has risen by 17 cm during the 20th century, in part because of the melting of snow and ice from many mountains and in the Polar regions. The temperatures of the last half century are unusual in comparison with those of at least the previous 1300 years. Environmental changes introduce new constraints and equations into the market. Already, GREEN has become a buzzword in the advertising arena and in the coming years, sustainability will be a major game changer in the way technology and markets will evolve.
- **Political/Social revolution:** Revolutions have occurred through human history and have resulted in major changes in culture, economy and socio-political institutions.

Calamity

Disasters—natural or manmade—can cause major turbulence at all levels—economic, social, political, environmental, etc., and thus need to be factored in while planning for exigencies.

- **Natural disaster:** A natural disaster is a major adverse event resulting from natural processes of the Earth. Examples are floods, droughts, hurricanes, tornadoes, volcanic eruptions, earthquakes, tsunamis and other geologic processes.
- **Epidemic:** An epidemic is the rapid spread of an infectious disease to a large number of people in a given population within a short period of time.
- **Accidents:** Losses caused due to fire or other types of accidents could be detrimental to any organisation.
- **War/Terrorism:** Wars have caused huge loss of life and property. World War II wiped out 3–5% of the world's population.

Conflict

In the world of cutthroat competition today, it is not surprising to be at the receiving end of inimical or deceitful behaviour from ones adversaries—both external and internal. Such conflicts may induce lot of uncertainty and change in the environment. Following are some of the possible scenarios which may arise due to interpersonal conflicts:

- Property/Legal dispute
- Financial malevolence

- Violence/assault
- Unfavourable establishment/government
- Public defamation through media

NAVIGATING UNCERTAINTY AND CHANGE

Navigating through seasons of uncertainty and change is akin to riding in a rocky mountainous terrain with uneven turf and unpredictable slopes. A normal luxury car would break down in such a terrain. You need a special sports utility vehicle (SUV) to take on the mountaineering challenge. Similarly, navigating uncertainty and change also warrants that a stable and robust organisational SUV is put in place. Secondly, you also need an expert driver who can manoeuver the vehicle skillfully. Similarly, you need an expert leader who can apply certain principles and processes to drive this vehicle through the fog of uncertainty and change. Essentially, we need to work on the following:

- Building a vehicle to navigate change and uncertainty
- Driving the vehicle through change and uncertainty

Building a Vehicle to Navigate Change and Uncertainty

Uncertainties can arise due to factors which are within our control and also due to factors which are beyond our control. Incorporating elements like resilient leadership, systems approach, communication protocols, succession planning, delegation and organisation culture helps create a robust organisational vehicle which can minimise the shocks of uncertainty and change. Let us look at some of the elements which can help create a resilient organisational vehicle to enable us to navigate the bumpy terrain of uncertainty and change:

- Mature and resilient leadership
- Proactive systems approach
- Communication protocols
- Succession planning and training
- Delegation and empowerment
- Embedding the right organisational culture

Mature and Resilient Leadership

Mature and resilient leadership serves as the strong foundation which helps the building of the organisation to absorb the tremors of change. History is witness to the fact that resilient leaders have shaped resilient nations and businesses. The glories of the Pandavas in the Mahabharata extends much further than just their unmatched military skills. Even more impressive than their military acumen was their ability to intelligently deal with uncomfortable and unpredictable circumstances. They repeatedly faced many perplexing situations such as the Kuru's frequent attempts to take their lives via poison or fire, to forfeiting everything they owned to an altered gambling match. Likewise, the chaste Draupadi had to withstand being disrobed in the Kuru assembly, being kidnapped by Jayadratha and Kichaka's attempted molestation. Moreover, despite his distinguished masculinity, Arjuna was even forced to cope with Urvashi's curse of losing his manhood but he used it to his advantage when the Pandavas were to go incognito in the final year of their exile. In the Yaksha Prashna episode, Yudhishtira turned the calamitous situation of the death of his four brothers into a boon of lifelong victory from Yamaraj by coolly and patiently answering the abstruse questions of Yaksha (Yamaraj in disguise). Thus, Yudhishtira's maturity and resilience and that of his brothers' was the key to their success despite all odds.

The life of American techno-entrepreneur, Steve Jobs, is another case in point. His own life went through winding lanes of ups and downs and his resilience in the face of it all, makes for a gripping account of personal and entrepreneurial success. After dropping out of Reed College, Jobs and his buddy Steve Wozniak launched Apple Computer from his family's garage in 1976.

Alan Deutschman, author of *Change or Die, The Second Coming of Steve Jobs*, tells us the tale of this legendary visionary of our times: 'He co-founds Apple Computer when he is 21, and by the time he is 23 he's a millionaire. He becomes legendary. And then, at 30, he has this humiliating defeat.'[19] Deutschman is referring to Jobs' expulsion from the company he founded after a power struggle with CEO, John Sculley, in 1985. In his famous 2005 Stanford speech, Jobs admitted, 'I really didn't know what to do for a few months (after the expulsion). I even thought about running away from Silicon Valley. But something slowly began to dawn on me. I still loved what I did. The turn of events at Apple had not changed that one bit. And so I decided to start over.'

However, turning the tables on failures and reversals is not an easy thing. It calls for great humility and courage—humility to accept one's shortcomings and learn from them and the courage to try once more. Jobs tied up with a former colleague and launched NeXT technologies. NeXT never became the success Jobs hoped it would be. However, his time at NeXT gave him the space to hone his abilities as a CEO. Meanwhile, Apple was losing its cutting edge and consequently its sales plummeted. The company lost $1.04 billion in the fiscal year of 1997. In 1996, Apple Computer acquired NeXT, returning Jobs to the company he helped create. The following year, Jobs became Apple's CEO and remarkably turned things around. He led the company out of the troughs of slump to the crests of its greatest successes, from the iPod to the iPhone to the iPad.

Sometimes, reversals in life can act as tipping points to lead us into realms of unprecedented growth and success. Jobs put it this way in his speech to Stanford graduates: 'I didn't see it then, but it turned out that getting fired from Apple was the best thing that could have ever happened to me. The heaviness of being successful was replaced by the lightness of being a beginner again, less sure about everything. It freed me to enter into one of the most creative periods of my life,' he said.

'I'm pretty sure none of this would have happened if I hadn't been fired from Apple. It was an awful tasting medicine, but I guess the patient needed it. Sometimes life hits you in the head with a brick. Don't lose faith. I'm convinced the only thing that kept me going was that I loved what I did. You've got to find what you love.'

Deutschman talks of the resilience of Jobs, 'He persisted, he has this incredible tenacity. He holds on and he comes back with triumph after triumph, driving this company to new heights, creating the greatest corporate success of our time. It's a unique story. I think he wanted to prove his early success at Apple wasn't a fluke, that he wasn't a kid who got lucky and was in the right place at the right time. The conventional wisdom was that Steve Jobs was a great visionary but not a good businessman. But in his second time at Apple he wasn't just a visionary. He made a point of learning how to be a great businessman.' Thus, those leaders who have demonstrated the ability to deal with uncertainty and change in their own lives, wield the mettle to steer their organisations through periods of uncertainty and change.

Proactive Systems Approach

Erecting a superstructure of pre-defined systems and processes eliminates undue uncertainties and frees you up to focus on only those uncertainties and changes which are inevitable or necessary. Following are characteristics of a system:

- A system is a whole composed of many parts (e.g., a car).
- The systemic unit has a definable purpose (e.g., a car's purpose is to provide personal transportation).
- Each part of the system has a defined role or function and contributes to the system's purpose (eg., car's engine, gearbox, etc.).
- The parts function in sequence and in parallel according to a design to fulfill the purpose of the system.

Proactive systems approach entails having documented answers to the following questions:

1. Why? Vision/Purpose
2. What? Goals/Strategy/Priority
3. Who? Roles/Job descriptions
4. How? Processes/Systems/Communication channels/Technology/Resources/Training
5. Where? Work environment/Organisational culture
6. What if? Backup plan/Crisis management

You can have a documentation team interview members of your organisation from top level to grassroots to get answers to the above questions.

Communication Protocols

A streamlined communication architecture within your organisation will help minimise the chaos and confusion caused by incumbent uncertainty and change. The new fault lines will be quickly detected and handled due to efficient coordination within the organisation. Ben Horowitz, author of *The Hard Thing about Hard Things*, says, that, 'The CEO's most important operational responsibility is designing and implementing the communication architecture for the company. Absent a well-designed communication architecture, information and ideas will stagnate and your company will become a bad place to work at.'

Building a communication protocol minimises communication gaps and ensures alignment at all levels. A communication protocol is a formal process that outlines the types of information to be communicated in the organisation, as well as identifying the person(s) responsible for communicating particular topics. The protocol also outlines the audience, frequency and suggested communication vehicles for each type of communication. The following is a typical format for communication protocols:

#	Message	Who Delivers	Venue/ Vehicle	Audience	Frequency
1	Strategic Plan	CEO	E-mail	All	Monthly, Quarterly, Annually
2					
3					

Succession Planning and Training

Leadership successions are critical junctures which can potentially introduce a lot of uncertainty and change in the system. Succession planning can thus help check another possible source of uncertainty. A good succession planning process in place ensures the longevity of the organisation and a lead time to inculcate desired skillsets in the successor. It is the responsibility of a leader to set a succession plan rolling well in time, to prepare able people to take over at times of changeover. This concern of a leader is reflected in Dashrath as he is thinking of crowning Rama as the king.

Succession planning means that the organisation regularly conducts developmental, support and search activities to ensure that the institution continues effectively when staff who occupy key roles leave, retire or are elevated to higher levels in the organisation. It is different from replacement hiring which is a response to a vacancy; whereas succession planning is a proactive process that addresses needs before they arise. It is helpful to draw a succession plan for each key role within the organisation.

Delegation and Empowerment

If the architecture of the organisation is such that all the decisions and processes have to funnel through the leader because the authority isn't distributed at all levels, it is a sure shot recipe for chaos in times of uncertainty and change. Uncertainty and change are scenarios where the traffic of doubts and decision making increases and if the authority isn't distributed evenly, it would create a decisional traffic jam at the end of the top leadership, giving rise to serious bottlenecks. Therefore, it is essential that authority is evenly distributed at all levels in the organisation through the process of delegation and empowerment. Please refer to 'Leadership 101' for more details on the process of delegation.

Embedding the Right Organisational Culture

Organisational culture consists of the norms, values, beliefs, expectations, behaviours and assumptions that exist in an organisation. In the event of uncertainty and change, right organisational culture acts as a:

- Shock absorber by absorbing the shocks of change and not letting them cause jerks to the organisation
- Lubricant by minimising the friction which may arise in times of uncertainty and change

A detailed note on the science of embedding the right culture in the organisation can be found in 'Leadership 101'.

Driving the Vehicle through Change and Uncertainty

Building a robust organisational vehicle by implementing the principles mentioned above shall definitely prepare and brace the organisation to better deal with uncertainty and change. But we also need to have a look at practical steps which need to be taken when uncertainty and change strike:

- Survey and assessment
- Ownership and accountability
- High value decision making
- Mature and open communication

Survey and Assessment

The first step in the wake of uncertainty and change is to take stock of the new situation. Asking structured questions can help take a stock of the situation:

- What has changed and what has not?
- In the new situation, what factors are still in our control and which are beyond our control?
- How long is the situation of uncertainty or change going to last?
- Are we fully equipped to deal with the situation?

- Are there any competency/communication/ culture gaps which need to be plugged?
- How can we fill those gaps?

Chanakya says that it is very important for a person to be well-informed by able advisors, in terms of the following: 'Coming to know what is known, definite strengthening of what has become known, removal of doubt in case of two possible alternatives, finding out the rest in a matter that is partly known—this can be achieved with the help of ministers.' (*Arthashastra* 1.15.20–21)

Ownership and Accountability

In times of uncertainty, the leader needs to hold the anchor from one end by taking ownership of the situation. This gesture of the leader gives lot of stability and confidence to the team. The whole team then gets committed and geared up to transform the situation of uncertainty into an opportunity. An interesting incident happened during the first launch of the Indian Satellite Launch Vehicle (SLV) by ISRO in 1979 which highlights an example of a leader who took ownership for a situation of failure and uncertainty and thus helped make his team to turn around the situation.

Dr A.P.J. Abdul Kalam was the project director of SLV mission and Prof. Satish Dhawan was the chairman of ISRO at that time. That was the first time India was building its own rocket launch vehicle in Sri Harikota,

India. After ten years of hard struggle, they were ready to launch their first experimental rocket 'Rohini Technology Payload' on 10 August 1979.

The countdown started and Dr Abdul Kalam along with six other experts were monitoring the launch anxiously. When it was four minutes before the satellite launch, the computer began to go through a checklist. One minute later, the computer program put the launch on hold; the display showed that some control components were not in order. Everyone was stunned, not knowing whether to proceed or not. The whole country was waiting for the good news.

The experts advised Dr Abdul Kalam to go ahead with the launch as they were confident about their calculations. The decision was Dr Kalam's to take and he decided to bypass the computer, switched to manual mode and launched the rocket. In the first stage, everything worked fine. In the second stage, a problem developed. Instead of the satellite going into orbit, the whole rocket system plunged into the Bay of Bengal. It was a big failure.

The world media was waiting to ask hard questions to the scientists in the press meet—why did they fail, weren't they fully prepared, how could they waste the hard earned money of poor people of India, what are they going to do now, shouldn't they scrap all plans for satellite research, etc.

Dr Kalam was very frightened to face the media as he had no answers to all these challenging questions.

Prof. Satish Dhawan chose to address the press meet and made Dr Kalam sit beside him. Prof. Dhawan accepted the blame for the failure but exuded confidence in his team's success in the next attempt. He said, 'We failed! But I have a very good trust in my team that next time we will be succeeding for sure.'

Next year, on 18 July 1980, the same team led by Dr Kalam successfully launched Rohini RS-1 into the orbit! The whole country was proud and cheered the success of the launch. Prof. Satish Dhawan congratulated Dr Kalam and the team and asked him to conduct the press conference that day! The rest is history as we know it. Dr Kalam led many more successful launches and became the 'Missile Man' of India. This would not have happened without what Prof. Satish Dhawan did on the day of failure. He took charge in a situation of complete uncertainty and dejection and demonstrated the courage to take on the challenge afresh. The ownership of Prof. Dhawan and the trust he showed in his team inspired them to attain success the very next year.

High Value Decision Making

Lee Iacocca, former president of Ford and Chrysler, once said, 'The one word that makes a good manager is decisiveness'. But being decisive is not that easy in scenarios with multiple options, lack of full information and increasing uncertainty. High value decision making is about being able to make reasonable choices in real time despite uncertainty.

The Panchatantra tells the tale of a jackal called Mahachataraka who was smart enough to make the right moves at lightning speed to ensure his survival in the competitive forest. One day, he found an elephant's body and was happy as it would be his food for many days. However, he was not able to bite into the thick hide of the elephant and was circling around the body when a lion came that way. The jackal humbly prostrated before the lion and said, 'My lord, I am your obedient servant. At your command, I am keeping a vigil on the body of the elephant. Please help yourself.'

The lion said, 'You know my friend, I do not eat something others have killed. You may take it as my gift to you.'

'I am touched by your magnanimity, my lord,' said the jackal.

After the lion had left, a tiger came to the scene. The jackal thought, 'I got rid of one menace through humility. How do I escape this fellow? He will not yield to any strategy I know. The only way of keeping him at bay is cunning. Let me try it.'

The jackal then went halfway to greet the tiger and said, 'O uncle, why are you entering this area of death? The lion has killed this elephant and asked me to keep watch on it. He has gone to take bath. Before going, he told me to inform him if any tiger happened to come here. He vowed to kill all the tigers because a long time ago a tiger had nibbled at an elephant he had killed. He told me that from that day on he had sworn to kill all tigers.'

These words frightened the tiger.

He told the jackal, 'Son, save my life. When the lion comes, don't tell him I had come this way. Please.'

On receiving assurance from the jackal, the tiger hurriedly left the scene. Then came a leopard.

The jackal thought, 'This fellow has strong and sharp teeth. I will persuade him to pierce the hide of the elephant.'

Addressing the leopard, the jackal said, 'My son, you have come this way after a long time. You seem to be hungry. Why don't you be my guest? See this elephant that a lion has killed. He has asked me to keep an eye on the body. So, have a feast before he returns.'

The leopard said, 'Uncle, how can I accept your invitation? If I want to live long, I should not touch this elephant. I will leave now.'

The jackal assured him, 'Don't worry, you go ahead. I will alert you when the lion comes.'

The leopard then began attacking the elephant and tore through the hide. After the leopard had ate some share of the flesh, the jackal cried, 'Run! The lion is coming!'

In this way, the jackal managed to get rid of the leopard too after having the hide cut open by acting in symbiosis with him. And then the jackal had his fill with joy. In today's competitive world, a leader may want to draw some astuteness from this jackal's prompt presence of mind and prudent decision making.

Let me also share with you a real-life case study

of high value decision making in a situation where an error would mean loss of lives. I am referring to the decision of Chesley Sullenberger, pilot of Flight 1549 who decided to land the plane on the Hudson River when its two engines lost power after a bird hit.

On 15 January 2009, U.S. Airways Flight 1549, an Airbus A320, took off from LaGuardia Airport with 150 passengers and 5 crew members, bound for Charlotte, NC. Three minutes into the flight, it struck a flock of Canada geese and lost power in both engines. Sullenberger radioed a mayday call to New York Terminal Radar Approach Control: 'This is Cactus 1539, hit birds. We've lost thrust on both engines. We're turning back towards LaGuardia.' Air traffic controller Patrick Harten told LaGuardia's tower to hold all departures and directed Sullenberger back to Runway 13. Sullenberger responded, 'Unable.' Sullenberger asked controllers for landing options in New Jersey, mentioning Teterboro Airport. Permission was given for Teterboro's Runway 1, but Sullenberger responded: 'We can't do it.... We're gonna be in the Hudson.'

The aircraft passed less than 900 feet above the George Washington Bridge. Sullenberger commanded over the cabin address system, 'Brace for impact,' and the flight attendants relayed the command to passengers. Meanwhile, air traffic controllers asked the Coast Guard to caution vessels in the Hudson and ask them to prepare to assist with rescue. About 90 seconds later, the plane made an unpowered ditching, descending southwards at about 125 knots (140 mph) into the middle of the North River section of the Hudson tidal estuary. Sullenberger opened the cockpit door and gave the order to evacuate. The crew began evacuating the passengers through the four over-wing window exits and into an inflatable slide/raft deployed from the front right passenger door. Finally, Sullenberger walked the cabin twice to confirm it was empty.

Though air controllers tried to divert the plane back to LaGuardia or a nearby airport in New Jersey, Captain Sullenberger made his intuitive calculations and decided that he could not safely land the plane in either of the airports and glided the plane into the Hudson River. Later, an enquiry was done by National Transportation Safety Board (NTSB) using flight simulators to test the possibility that the flight could have returned safely to LaGuardia or diverted to Teterboro. The report confirmed that Sullenberger had made the right decision in split seconds under pressure. On 4 May 2010, the NTSB issued its final report, which identified the probable cause as 'the ingestion of large birds into each engine, which resulted in an almost total loss of thrust in both engines'. The final report credited the outcome to four factors: good decision-making and teamwork by the cockpit crew (including decisions to land in the Hudson); the fact that the A320 carried life vests and additional rafts even though not required for that route; the performance of the flight crew during the evacuation; and the proximity of working vessels to the ditching site. Though it may be outrageous to expect that we may be able to do such heroic and expeditious decision making every time, we can definitely brace ourselves for the unexpected by understanding the dynamics underlying such turbulent situations.

Mature & Open Communication

Change is inevitable—sometimes it is introduced by external factors but sometimes it is intentionally induced by the leadership for good. Handling any sort of change requires the organisation to change and adapt to the new situation. However, if an organisation has to change or adapt, it is the people within the organisation who have to change or adapt. And this is the tough part of the problem. Not everyone will be receptive to change. There will be wide ranging responses: affiliative, appreciative, accommodative, apprehensive and antagonistic. A story from the Panchatantra makes for an interesting read in this regard.

In a lake, there lived three fish who were long standing friends. The first fish had foresight and an open mind, the second one wasn't as open-minded but was smart enough to find a way out when in trouble, but the third was adamant and averse to changes. One day the fish saw a group of fishermen visit and overheard their conversation about earning a fortune by fishing in the lake. Sensing danger, the first cautioned his friends to move out of the lake, 'Haven't you heard what the fishermen were saying? We must move out of this pond tonight itself. As the wise men have said weak men should flee when a strong man invades or seeks refuge in a fort. There is no alternative. Let's go elsewhere. Those who are afraid of foreign lands and those who are bound to their soil will die in their own country. He who can prosper anywhere does not die in his own land clinging to sentiment.' The second fish said, 'There definitely is the probability of some danger here, but it seems preposterous to take such a drastic step immediately. I will stay here and find a way out if I'm caught.' The third fish said, 'I do not want to move out. Only an ungrateful fool will abandon the land of one's birth. I will remain here come what may. If I am destined to get caught, it will be so even if I go elsewhere.' The first fish moved out. The next day, the fisherman arrived and caught the other two fish. The second one cleverly escaped by pretending to be dead. The third fish did nothing and got caught and died.

The story showed us the diverse responses to the same situation by the three fish. Similarly, an organisation will witness several shades of responses in the face of change. Influencing and inspiring the people within the organisation to adapt as per the needs of the time is a great science. In general, human nature tends to search for a comfort zone and is often skeptical of change. This tendency brings about resistance to change. But it is the duty of the sponsors of change within the organisation to sensitively deal with the different shades of responses and help them become participative. Let us look at some of the principles and practices which can help swing the ticker from antagonistic to participative.

What All Should be Communicated to Orient People for the Change?

In the wake of a proposed change, the sponsors of change have the duty to communicate effectively so as to allay the doubts and fear surrounding the change and encourage everyone to participate in the change. Following are five important communication points surrounding any change:

- **Rationale:** Why is the change occurring?
- **Vision:** What will the organisation look like in the future?
- **Plan:** How and when does the organisation plan to make these changes?
- **Impetus:** Why should they support the change/ how will they benefit?
- **Support:** Who is supporting the change? What resources are being allocated?

Who All Should be Involved in the Change?

Does everyone in the organisation need to be consulted or involved in the change? Only the stakeholders need to be taken onboard. A classic definition of a stakeholder is a person who will be affected by the change and/or whose active support, commitment and behavioural change are required for successful implementation and sustained change.

Further, not all changes are significant enough to consult or involve all the stakeholders. For minute changes, it will suffice to just inform the stakeholders about the proposed or incumbent change. If everyone is involved in minor changes, it will be tantamount to wasting valuable collective time for the trivial and create a chaotic situation. In case of more significant changes, it would be more appropriate to consult the stakeholders and take their suggestions. Not all suggestions need be incorporated but it is important to clarify why certain suggestions have not been incorporated or have been postponed. For more serious changes, stakeholders need to be included in the discussions related to the change process which means the change and the change process should emerge based on the discussions. For major transformations, stakeholders need to be involved in the change process, i.e., they should be given important decision making and executive powers in the change process. Or else there could be major disapproval, resistance and roadblocks while execution.

How Should the Change Behaviour be Facilitated?

The knee-jerk reaction to any proposed change could be denial or resistance. As discussed previously, there could be wide ranging responses from different quarters to a change: affiliative, appreciative, accommodative, apprehensive and antagonistic. The table on the next page gives a list of typical responses and the corresponding facilitative approaches which the change sponsors may need to undertake to address the concerns and facilitate the change process.

The associated behaviours mentioned above is the language which can help you decipher where your stakeholders are with respect to the change. Based on where they are, you can engage in facilitative approaches to help the organization evolve through the change curve- from antagonistic to affiliative. Taking the stakeholders through this evolutionary journey may mean investment of lot of time and efforts but this shall ensure that the change is holistic and sustainable. Please note that understanding your stakeholders and incorporating their inputs is not only essential for taking them up the change curve but also for refining and fine-tuning the change itself. The wisdom of the team helps the change sponsors to go through a learning curve which helps in making the change more efficient and effective.

#	Response	Associated Behaviours	Facilitative Approaches
I	Antagonistic	*What you hear:* • This can't be, it is impossible. • It will never work. • We will not allow this to happen. • They are scheming against us. *What you see:* • Denial • Blame • Opposition/Defiance • Boycott • Activism/Lobbying	• Information dissemination • Trust-building exercises • Making trustworthy people the face for change • Addressing rumors and misinformation • Clarifying what is changing and what is not

#	Response	Associated Behaviours	Facilitative Approaches
2	Apprehensive	*What you hear:* • Why change? It used to be better before. • It might be harmful. • What are their real intentions? *What you see:* • Doubts/Skepticism • Withdrawal • Non-cooperation	• Orientation programs • Inviting suggestions • Active listening • Addressing concerns with empathy • Demonstrating results with small and non-binding pilots

#	Response	Associated Behaviours	Facilitative Approaches
3	Accommodative	*What you hear:* • What is in it for me? • I am ok either way. • No harm in trying out. • I hope more changes are not in store. *What you see:* • Inquiry • Tentativeness • Non-committal/Neutral • Exploration	• Involvement in discussions/negotiations • Brainstorming sessions • Training to bridge competency/attitude gaps
4	Appreciative	*What you hear:* • This might be better. • Where do we begin? • What can I do? *What you see:* • Cooperation • Participation	• Planning and executing meetings • Set short-term goals • Celebrating small wins

#	Response	Associated Behaviours	Facilitative Approaches
5	Affiliative	*What you hear:* • Excitement about the new opportunities. • Let's make it work. • I have got an idea. *What you see:* • Commitment • Ownership/Initiative • Teamwork • Innovation	• Coordinated efforts • Delegation • Rewarding innovation

9. WORK-LIFE BALANCE

Transform the Tightrope Walking of Multiple Responsibilities into a Cakewalk

Have you ever been in a flight which went through some turbulence either due to bad weather conditions or some technical snag? If so, you know how scary it can be. At 40,000 feet above the ground, the plane cannot afford to lose balance. I had been in one such flight which was passing through a thunderstorm near Mumbai airport. The plane was quaking and some cabin baggage started tumbling down. There was pin-drop silence in the aircraft as everyone sat tight with their seatbelts fastened—some praying, some biting their nails and some looking out the window. Thankfully, the technology of aerodynamic motions has developed several mechanisms to keep the plane balanced despite turbulent conditions. The aircraft employs elements such as ailerons, rudder and tail-plane or elevator to manoeuver against any asymmetric forces, so that the aircraft can balance the movement in the roll, yaw and pitch axes.[20] Thankfully the pilots of our airplane managed the situation well and the plane landed in a short while, much to the respite of the anxious passengers.

While we cruise through the journey of our life, we might come across bad weather conditions such as some setback or crisis in terms of finances, profession or relationships or may develop some technical snag such as some illness at the physical or emotional levels. Do we have inbuilt mechanisms to keep the plane of our life balanced even in such turbulent conditions of life? If not, the consequences could be disastrous. But if we have these balancing mechanisms installed in the plane of our life, we could be cruising through at high altitudes and at great speeds without any anxiety or fear. With this background let us talk about some of the balancing mechanisms in the aircraft of life.

The aircraft of our life can rotate about three axes:

1. **Connection;** Personal life
2. **Community:** Interpersonal life
3. **Contribution:** Professional life

Any imbalance in any of these three axes could result in unwanted turbulence in our life. I will use the analogy of the tree of life to explain the function of each of the three axes of life. Connection to self and God forms the invisible roots of the tree of life. The roots are invisible but that's where the juice and nourishment are coming from. Because the roots are invisible, often there may be a tendency to neglect them and focus on the visible fruits but if the roots are neglected for long, there eventually won't be any fruits either. If the roots are not deep and strong, winds of change can topple the entire tree upside down. Community, i.e., healthy relationships, form the trunk of the tree of life. Being in the middle, the tree is connected to both the roots and the crown and is central to the health of both which means that if we have a compromised social life, our spiritual health and our contribution to the world will both be impacted. Finally, our contribution to the society through our professional or philanthropic activities represents the crown in the tree of life, which contains the branches, leaves and fruits. It is the most visible and coveted portion of the tree. The ultimate purpose which the tree serves comes from the crown—it provides shade to people from the sun and succulent fruits for people to eat. However, you cannot obtain good fruits without strong roots and healthy trunk. In other words, one cannot be a good contributor without having deep spiritual roots and healthy relationships. Thus, we see that all three are interdependent on each other.

CONNECTION: PERSONAL LIFE

Most of us ensure that our phones and other essential gadgets are fully charged up before we step out of home in the morning. In the same way, do we take time out to charge ourselves physically, mentally and spiritually before we embark on the challenges of the world outside, which can soon drain out our limited stock of energy? When you are operating on low battery, any demands from the external environment can lead to a breakdown or a blast, just as your phone dies or heats up if you have been on a long Zoom call without sufficient charge. Therefore, it is essential that we take some time in the day to charge ourselves—physically, mentally and spiritually. You can call this time 'Me Time', the time you have reserved to invest exclusively in yourself. Morning is the ideal time to give yourself an edge before interacting with the world. Basically, this is the time you connect with your body, mind, soul and God.

What can I do to connect and charge myself? There is a plethora of activities which can charge our batteries. Let me share a basic outline. Generally, the first thing we do after waking up is to either brood on the things we did yesterday and ponder on what went well and what didn't. Or else we make a mental list of the things which we are supposed to do today. Or else we check our phone for notifications. However, with this approach we are pushing ourselves into the mode of passion which is characterised by frenzy, craving and frustration. Instead, if you spend a few minutes contemplating upon your purpose and the type of person you want to be today, you could enter a state of self-awareness and thus live your day as a human being and not a human doing.

The practice of meditation should be a part of one's daily routine. It helps us become focused and spiritually charged up. Clinical studies have shown that meditation reduces levels of stress, depression and anxiety and also reverses the harmful effects caused by them.[21] There are other practices such as journal writing or prayer which some people include in their morning schedule. These spiritual practices could be followed up by charging up the body too by doing some *asanas* or workout or going for a jog or brisk walk or a nature walk. Investing an hour or so in the above activities will not only refresh you spiritually but also rejuvenate your body and mind. Eventually, you will figure out that it makes you more effective and efficient in whatever you do during the day and leaves you with a happy experience of life. However, the key to successfully and sustainably doing these morning routines is to sleep early at night.

COMMUNITY: INTERPERSONAL LIFE

The next axis is the community axis which is about a healthy social life, especially deep meaningful relationships with a few close family members and friends. Satisfaction is experience through fulfillment of the heart and not through fulfillment of the ego. It is relationships which fill the heart and not achievements. It is very important for any individual to have holistic 360^0 relationships. Just as a wholesome meal has variegated smells, tastes and flavours, a wholesome personality needs holistic relationships. A human being has three needs in terms of relationships:

1. Accountability: Need to feel accountable to and be cared for by someone (Seniors)
2. Responsibility: Need to feel responsible for and care for someone (Juniors)
3. Affection: Need to have affectionate exchanges with someone (Equals)

An ideal family provides for fulfillment of all these needs:

1. There are parents and superiors who guide us and we feel a sense of accountability towards them for our actions.
2. There are children and younger members for whom we feel concerned and responsible.
3. There is a spouse, siblings and friends with whom we can openly exchange our hearts, struggles and aspirations.

We need to knit such a community around us where we are having exchanges at all these three levels. Rupa Goswami, one of the great Bhakti saints of the 16th century, reveals three secrets for developing deep meaningful relationships:

- **Exchange of loving service:** Accepting service is as important as offering service in a relationship. The self-esteem of some people may come in the way of accepting service from others. They may send signals that 'I am alright and I don't need your help please.' When someone comes to offer help and care but is turned away, they may feel slighted or unwanted. The person offering help will feel discouraged to offer further help in future. We should accept with deep gratitude any gesture of help or care that may come our way. We can later reciprocate by rendering service to them at an appropriate time. After all, life is all about giving and receiving.

- **Confidential and meaningful dialogue:** A part of forming deep bonds is to become vulnerable in front of our loved ones and accept their vulnerabilities without judgement too. Such conversations have the power to heal wounded hearts and fill the heart with the nectar of love.
- **Eating food together:** The way to a man's heart is through his stomach. We are what we eat and it seems that when we eat together, we grow together and bond together in a very special way.

Generally, evenings are the time for community. You could call this time 'We Time', i.e., the time you choose to keep everything aside to be fully present with your loved ones in all their highs and lows, hopes and horrors, joys and sorrows.

CONTRIBUTION: PROFESSIONAL LIFE

The third axis is the contribution axis which represents our contribution to the world through profession or philanthropy or activism. Each one of us has been gifted with some special talents by God to be utilised to serve the society in a unique way. Playing a small part in an active meaningful mission or a purpose-driven organisation gives one a sense of self-worth, community and purpose.

Flowing water remains fresh and pure, whereas stagnant water becomes polluted and contaminated. Similarly, a person who is actively engaged in a meaningful mission and is upgrading their skills and takings up newer challenges remains fresh and lively whereas a person who chooses to remain in their comfort zone and is not engaged as per their capabilities becomes stagnant and cranky. Therefore, it is essential that we find suitably challenging engagements for ourselves at all stages of life. The day is the obvious time which is reserved for contribution. You could call it 'Work Time', the time reserved for making a difference in a field that matters to you.

HEDGING YOUR INVESTMENTS

Your time is your greatest asset and how you invest your time practically determines everything in your life. Good investors are known to hedge their investments among multiple instruments in such a way that maximises the returns and minimises the risks. Having seen that connection, community and contribution are three sacred aspects of our life, we need to invest in all of them consciously, so that the aircraft of our life maintains its balance and sails through despite external turbulences.

The connection or the spiritual and self-growth aspect of your life is like government bonds: no risk but slow returns. There is practically no risk involved here but the returns can be reaped only after a period of time. You cannot expect to change yourself overnight with mindfulness practices but with regular practice you will gradually be able to see marked improvements in yourself.

The contribution dimension of life is the most volatile one. You could compare it to equity or stock markets: high risks but high returns. If you are hard-working and enterprising, you could build an empire for yourself in no time in terms of fortune, fame or followers, but the volatile nature of the world ensures that those who are up come down and those who are down go up.

The community part of your life is somewhere in between the two, more like mutual funds: medium risks and medium returns. Deep relationships require sustained investment for long periods of time but then once they become mature, they become so valuable that you would not trade them for any wealth in this world. However, improper understanding of relationships and undue expectations can cause the relationships to grow sour and cause heartburns.

A rookie investor may get tempted to invest all their wealth in one instrument which may appear very lucrative. However, a mature investor creates a diverse portfolio. Similarly, we need to create a diverse portfolio for our life by investing equally in all three dimensions—connection, community and contribution. Suppose if you invest all your time, energy and resources only in one of these three buckets and later find out that the bucket developed a crack or a hole and all your investment has leaked out, wouldn't you feel crestfallen and dejected? So, the smart way is to hedge your investment among these three buckets.

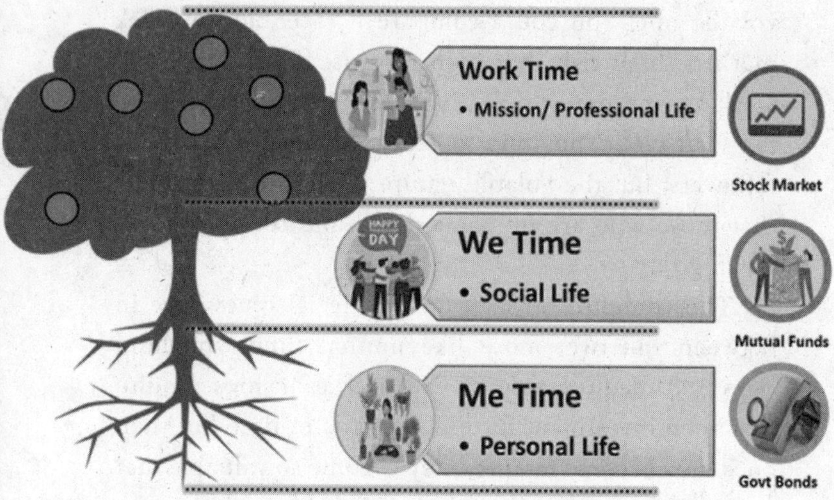

WORK-LIFE BALANCE: ACTIVITY 1

Balanced Scorecard for Life

What you do not measure, you cannot improve. The following is a monthly goal-setting tool which helps you set goals for things that matter in your life. For each of the areas mentioned below, write down what would be a measure of success by which you would gauge your progress or performance in the area. After laying out your success measures, set goals for yourself for the month in the identified area.

MONTH: **YEAR:**

Area	Measure of Success	SMART Goal	Frequency
Contribution-Professional/ Mission			
Community-Relationships			
Connection- Health & Well-Being			
Connection-Spiritual			

References

1. Bill Tym. *Five Reasons Why Novak Djokovic Rules Men's Tennis.* https://www.tennistakes.com/five-reasons-why-novak-djokovic-rules-mens-tennis/
2. https://humanengineers.com/success-is-in-helping-others-to-win/
3. https://www.nbcnews.com/better/relationships/survival-fittest-has-evolved-try-survival-kindest-n730196
4. Mehrabian, Albert. *Silent Messages* (1st ed.). Belmont, CA: Wadsworth, 1971. ISBN 0-534-00910-7
5. Morgan Nick. *7 Surprising Truths about Body Language*, Forbes Article on Body Language. https://www.forbes.com/sites/nickmorgan/2012/10/25/7-surprising-truths-about-body-language/#49df3651509f
6. David W. Angel, *The Four Types of Conversations.* Medium blog, Dec 2016. Available At: https://medium.com/@DavidWAngel/the-four-types-of-conversations-debate-dialogue-discourse-and-diatribe-898d19ecccoa
7. Jon R. Katzenbach , Douglas K. Smith. *The Wisdom*

of Teams: Creating the High-Performance Organization. Harvard Business Review Press, 2015. ISBN-10: 9781633691063.

8. Sumbramanian Kalpathi. *Lessons from the Cockpit*. https://www.knolskape.com/blog-lessons-from-the-cockpit-how-embracing-collaboration-at-the-top-can-eliminate-in-flight-errors/
9. Tuckman, Bruce W. 'Developmental sequence in small groups' in *Psychological Bulletin*, 1965. 63 (6): 384–399. doi:10.1037/h0022100. PMID 14314073.
10. Maria Trimarchi, '10 of the Worst Decisions Ever Made', Article on howstuffworks portal, https://history.howstuffworks.com/historical-events/10-worst-decisions.htm
11. LexisNexis International Workplace Productivity Survey, 2010, http://www.multivu.com/players/English/46619-LexisNexis-International-Workplace-Productivity-Survey/flexSwf/impAsset/document/9df84f1b-4525-4db9-b4ea-5dda5f6c3937.pdf
12. Gorman Brian. *Change Leadership: Why Your Head, Heart And Gut Are Critical To Listen To*, Forbes Magazine, Mar 2019. Available at: https://www.forbes.com/sites/forbescoachescouncil/2019/03/04/change-leadership-why-your-head-heart-and-gut-are-critical-to-listen-to/?sh=6405d58a4a96
13. John C Maxwell. *Developing the Leader within You*. Thomas Nelson Publishing; 1 edition (April 6, 2012). ISBN-10: 0785281126
14. Tosti, D.T. *How to Get the Culture You Need*. ISPI Journal, Jan 2007 ed

15. Research on Workplace Culture by Deloitte, Available At: https://www2.deloitte.com/content/dam/Deloitte/global/Documents/About-Deloitte/gx-core-beliefs-and-culture.pdf
16. Edgar Schein, *Organizational Culture & Leadership*. Wiley; Fifth edition, 2017. ISBN-10: 8126566671
17. Donald L. Kirkpatrick and James D. Kirkpatrick, *Evaluating Training Programs: The Four Levels*. Berrett-Koehler, 1st Edition, 1993.
18. Heather Boushey and Sarah Glynn. *There Are Significant Business Costs to Replacing Employees*, americanprogress.org. Available at: https://www.americanprogress.org/issues/economy/reports/2012/11/16/44464/there-are-significant-business-costs-to-replacing-employees/
19. Joel Siegel. *When Steve Jobs Got Fired By Apple*. https://abcnews.go.com/Technology/steve-jobs-fire-company/story?id=14683754
20. https://howthingsfly.si.edu/media/roll-pitch-yaw
21. Matthew Thorpe, MD, PhD and Rachael Link, MS. 12 Science-Based Benefits of Meditation, Healthline. Available at: https://www.healthline.com/nutrition/12-benefits-of-meditation#1.-Reduces-stress

Acknowledgements

In the Bhagavad Gita, Lord Krishna says that behind success in any endeavor, there are 5 factors involved—the environment around, the equipment used, the efforts put, the executor and ultimately the endorsement of God. This book is no different. Many people have directly and indirectly contributed to the production of this book through either of efforts, enlightenment or encouragement. I would like to express my gratitude to each one of them and offer this work as an ode to what they have done to shape me and this book.

Special thanks are due to the editing team at the Simon and Schuster—Himanjali Sankar, and Elizabeth—whose painstaking efforts have brought out the book in its present form. Also I am very grateful to the Commissioning Editor Sayantan Ghosh and MD CEO Rahul Srivastava for placing their trust in me and confidence in this book and investing in it.

And last but not the least, my heartfelt thanks to all

of you readers for giving me an opportunity to connect to you and serve you through this book.

Rasikraman Das
3 July 2023, Guru Purnima
Mumbai

About the Author

Rasikraman Das is a monk, author and life-coach. Being a gold-medalist in engineering and an M.Tech from IIT Bombay with rich experience as a monk and life coach at ISKCON, he brings to the table a unique blend of new-age scientific temper and age-old traditional wisdom.

He is the Founder Director of InPlug Academy which aims to empower the youth with essential life skills and create successful and fulfilled individuals, communities and organisations. He is also a professor at Dr Vivek Bindra's Bada Business. With a keen interest in the field of training and education, he has been instrumental in developing the Bhaktivedanta Vidyapitha Research Center (affiliated to Mumbai University) and has served in various capacities with the Organisational Development Committee of ISKCON GBC. He is also an associate faculty with the GBC College for Leadership Development, which imparts training in spiritual leadership.

Rasikraman Das also conducts leadership and life-skills workshops for students and working professionals. He has authored two other books—*Be the Smarter You: Your Appstore for Success and Happiness* which aims at equipping individuals with skills for self-growth and interpersonal synergy and *Being Srila Prabhupada-Anugas*, which is a handbook of spiritual leadership based on the life and teachings of ISKCON's founder-acharya, Srila Prabhupada, and has now been translated in several languages like Chinese, Russian etc.

Author Contact Information:

https://linktr.ee/Rasikramandas
Website: https://www.inplug.org/
Email: rasikraman.rns@gmail.com
https://www.linkedin.com/in/rasikraman
https://www.instagram.com/rasikraman/
https://www.youtube.com/@rasikraman/
https://twitter.com/RamanRasik
https://www.facebook.com/rasikramandas/